Purposeful Discussions

Geoff Hudson-Searle

Matador
9 Priory Business Park,
Wistow Road,
Kibworth Beauchamp,
Leicestershire. LE8 0RX
Tel: (+44) 116 279 2299
Email: books@troubador.co.uk
Web: www.troubador.co.uk/matador

ISBN (Paperback) 978 1838593 285
ISBN (Hardback) 978 1838593 292

British Library Cataloguing in Publication Data.
A catalogue record for this book is available from the British Library.

Typeset in 11pt Aldine401 BT by Troubador Publishing Ltd, Leicester, UK
Printed and bound in the UK by TJ International, Padstow, Cornwall

Matador is an imprint of Troubador Publishing Ltd

I would like to thank my wonderful wife Mary-Ann, and wonderful friends Mark and Jackie, and Sophie, who allowed me to dream and never stopped believing in this book. Without their love, support and constant belief, Purposeful Discussions would not have been possible.

CONTENTS

Preface   ix

PART ONE   **Communication**   **1**

1. Leadership in the digital world   3

2. Why we need to set high standards to be extraordinary   9

3. Are we really understanding our customers
   or ignoring the facts?   14

4. Why are our human-to-human relationships
   so disconnected from real life?   18

5. More management, more leaders – or are we failing in business?   25

6. How can a meaningful conversation help your business?   29

7. Purposeful driven discussions with Mark Herbert   33

8. The tide is rising on the fourth industrial revolution   37

PART TWO   **Strategy**   **43**

9.   So exactly how do we value time?   45

10. Is customer loyalty sustainable in today's digital world?   52

11. The extraordinary life of challenging the status quo   59

12. The challenges of leadership and digital disruption   64

13. Parallels between corporate environments and hummingbirds   71

14. Why forecasting is important   76

15. Why corporate governance should not
     be stored on your C drive   82

16. Not enough time… too much work   88

17. Does your executive board need an entrepreneurial
     approach to business?   93

18. Does (and should) shareholder value rule business?   100

19. What is required to be an effective leader in today's
     totally disruptive business world?   109

20. Have we forgotten leadership and the foundation
     of business planning?   113

21. Why leadership matters   118

PART THREE **Company growth and planning** **125**

22. Quantity or quality? 127

23. If you can tweet, you can become president 132

24. Is the world really out of control? 139

25. Do we have international differences in
    corporate governance and conduct? 143

26. Exactly what is the future in technology? 153

27. How to infuse boards with entrepreneurial spirit 158

28. Not just data… meaningful data that enables decisions 165

29. What can we all learn from the cyber threat landscape
    of 2020 and beyond? 171

30. Disruptive change is inevitable – change is constant 183

31. Will globalisation actually happen? 189

32. The keys to fulfilment: determination and perseverance 195

Epilogue 200

About Geoff Hudson-Searle 209

PREFACE

'The way we communicate with others and with ourselves ultimately determines the quality of our lives' – life coach
Anthony Robbins

This book has been written about very passionate subjects in business today – communication, strategy, and business development and life growth – which are essential for success and profitability in the business process.

In February 2014 I set out to write a weekly blog across a variety of subjects, especially people in business, opinions, research and tips, as well as some revelations that occurred to me. This is the second book I have written based on those blogs and themes, and it demonstrates the relationship between strategy, business development and life growth. It is important to understand that a number of the ideas, developments and techniques employed at the beginning as well as the top of business can be applied all across a company or life situation.

Purposeful Discussions provides a holistic overview of the essential leading methods in these areas, and can be viewed as a hands-on guide. Readers will gain insights into topical subjects, including a wide range of tips, models and techniques that will help to build strong and effective solutions in today's business world. One Amazon reviewer said of one of my previous publications, *Meaningful Conversations,* which worked in a similar way: "What makes a book remarkable, useful and meaningful for professionals? Well, read (not only once) Geoff's masterpiece and you will understand. This book is my 'win book' from so many aspects."

The terms 'communication', 'strategy', and 'business development and growth' have been overused during the last decade and devalued as a result. In this book, I aim to simplify these terms and to re-value management and leadership by addressing topics and subjects in each chapter. The book is divided into three key areas to make it easy to find the material you need. Each component can be located by the titles at the top of the pages. The sections within the three components relate strongly to each other and are interrelated to all the other sections. You can start with your particular area of interest, or you can read the book from the first page to the end; there really is a topic for everyone.

Business professionals and individuals dealing with the great challenges of today's business world have renewed responsibility for what business does best: innovate, invest and grow. Many people wait until circumstances force change and transformation, which can be radical and painful; this book will arm you with tips, advice and techniques to provide fresh thinking about your everyday environment and inspire innovation within your circumstances to create a better environment. We are all extraordinary people and have the ability to share and provide wealth creation and richness to our surroundings. The question is, how much do we want to be extraordinary?

Purposeful Discussions has been written not just for people in a company or organisation. It aims to support understanding across a wide variety of subjects for all kinds of people: students, budding entrepreneurs, business people and anyone who aspires to do better.

PART ONE

Communication

PART ONE

Communication

CHAPTER ONE

Leadership in the digital world

'Leadership is not about a title or a designation. It's about impact, influence and inspiration. Impact involves getting results, influence is about spreading the passion you have for your work, and you have to inspire teammates and customers'
– lawyer and writer Robin S Sharma

The Christmas holiday period is always a good time for reflection. Last year I spent it in Arizona, in the United States, and, once my dreaded cold had calmed down, I started to reflect on some of the most influential push buttons of business, and 'leadership' firmly came to mind.

I had decided to go for a hike and picked Sabino Canyon, a significant canyon located in the Santa Catalina Mountains and the Coronado National Forest north of Tucson. Sabino Canyon is a popular recreation area for residents of and visitors to Southern Arizona, providing a place to walk, hike or ride. Minutes away from the desert are large waterfalls along Sabino Creek, with minor bridges constructed over them. Wildlife in the canyon includes deer, pig-like javelina, skunks, tortoises, rattlesnakes and mountain lions.

As I started to climb this magnificent caynon, I thought about the new millennium and the Information Age that is setting the stage for a changing world. Social scientist Thalia Wheatley states that information is a dynamic element that gives way to order, growth and defines what is alive. It is from this fluid movement of information that we get change. "This is the world of Darwin, where we have to change to survive; where we have to develop to thrive; and paradoxically, where the very act of change increases the risk that we will not survive.

Ours is now a world of mergers, downsizing, reorganisation, diversity and more women in the workplace.

My understanding of leadership is that it is the ability to motivate groups of people towards a common goal, an incredibly important skill in the business world. Without strong leadership, many otherwise good businesses fail. Understanding the characteristics of strong leaders and cultivating those skills is paramount for those pursing a career in business.

Many of the world's most respected leaders have several personality traits in common. Some of the most recognisable traits are the ability to initiate change and inspire a shared vision, as well as knowing how to 'encourage the heart' and model the skills and behaviours that are necessary to achieve the stated objectives. Good leaders must also be confident enough in themselves to enable others to contribute and succeed.

Let's look at some of the most recognised model leaders from the past:

Franklin D Roosevelt – the ability to initiate change

Good leaders are never satisfied with the status quo and usually take action to change it.

In addition, strong leaders bring about change for the common good by involving others in the process. Roosevelt sought practical ways to help struggling men and women make a better world for themselves and their children. His philosophy involved "bold, persistent experimentation". "Take a method and try it," he said. "If it fails, admit it frankly and try another. But above all, try something." Being willing to take risks by trying new ideas and involving others in the process of change is a key quality of strong leaders.

Martin Luther King – inspiring a shared vision

Leaders, through their words and actions, must have the ability to draw others in to a common vision by telling others where they intend to go and urging them to join in that vision. Martin Luther King's vision of a country free from racial segregation and discrimination, so poignantly expressed in his famous "I have a dream" speech, exemplifies this critical leadership trait. He had a vision of a better America, and his ability to bring both whites and blacks together to march against segregation changed America profoundly.

Strong leaders not only need to have a vision and the ability to initiate change, they must model the values, actions and behaviours necessary to make the vision reality.

Mohandas K Ghandi – model leadership

Ghandi not only created and espoused the philosophies of passive resistance and constructive non-violence, he lived by these principles. According to former Indian prime minister Indira Gandhi, "More than his words, his life was his message." By choosing to consistently live and work in a manner that epitomised the values he believed in, Ghandi engendered trust, becoming a role model for others looking to effect change without resorting to violence.

Winston Churchill – encouraging the heart

On December 29, 1940, London was hit by one of the largest aerial attacks of the Second World War. Somehow, St Paul's Cathedral survived. Two days later a photo showing a silhouette of the dome of St Paul's surrounded by smoke and flames ran in the newspaper with a caption that read, "It symbolises the steadiness of London's stand against the enemy: the firmness of right against wrong". Prime minister Winston Churchill was a leader who encouraged the heart. He recognised the importance of St Paul's as a morale booster. His instructions were clear on that December night: "At all costs, St Paul's must be saved." Leaders must be able to encourage the hearts of those who share their vision, providing a sense of confident optimism even in the face of enormous difficulties.

These traditional leadership skills are still relevant today, but now, in this Information Age, they must co-exist with a mix of new factors.

First of all, digital leadership can be defined by the contribution a leader makes to a knowledge society or community and people's knowledge of technology. A knowledge society is one in which digital leaders have an obligation to keep up with the ongoing global revolution. They must understand technology, not merely as an enabler but also for its revolutionary force.

Leadership must be driven by an attitude of openness and a genuine hunger for knowledge. Of course, no rule dictates that leaders must be literate in coding, or that they should graduate in machine learning, but there is an imperative to understand the impact of breakthrough or revolutionary technologies.

Today's leaders must have the ability to identify technological trends across different sectors, such as big data, cloud computing, automation, and robotics. However, they must possess sufficient knowledge and the vision to be able to use these resources most effectively.

Secondly, in a knowledge society, what we do not know is as important as what we do know. Leaders should know their limits and know how to acquire missing knowledge. A leader of the future is more like a community manager rather than an authoritarian.

These days, we are seeing the decline of traditional hierarchical models of organisation. Take a look at how the organisation of governments has changed across Western societies in recent years. A number have introduced or reinforced public consultation processes as well as opened up public data for the benefit of their citizens.

These processes, by and large, will continue to grow. As a result, the hierarchical model tends to be suppressed and replaced by horizontal structures among executives, leaders from different sectors, researchers, and representatives from civic society.

Hierarchy fails in the digital age because it is slow and bureaucratic, whereas the new world is constantly changing and requires immediate responses.

As I descended from this amazing hike through the Canyon I started to think about the importance of information. In today's world, power is not gained by expanding new territories or areas of influence, but by deepening and widening networks and connections. But what is the role of the individual or leader, or of qualities that distinguish one grain of sand from another?

Having acknowledged that digital technology will play a decisive role our future, leaders cannot afford to show fear or reluctance in implementing it. Instead, they must embrace technology with a clear view of its potential. We must set sail for new, ambitious lands. We choose to go to Mars because our technology enables us to at least attempt the exploration of other planets by the 2030s. And we choose to develop other fantastic things every day – self-driving cars, more powerful batteries, the Apple Watch, drones, to name just a few.

Leadership in today's world is a balanced mix of universal characteristics and digital leadership traits which has the potential to guide us through years of transformation with optimism and idealism. Technology continues to prove that it can be used for the benefit of humanity, but only if we set sail on the right course led by smart individuals that make our journey, progress, and performance worthwhile.

CHAPTER TWO

Why we need to set high standards to be extraordinary

'Any time you sincerely want to make a change, the first thing you must do is to raise your standards'
– life coach Anthony Robbins

I had coffee with a good friend and journalist recently, and we discussed my book *Meaningful Conversations,* excellence and being extraordinary in life. We also talked about Darwin and the contribution his research and study of nature has made to business today. All of our discussions had one fundamental commonality: to be extraordinary, you need to set high standards and have a purpose.

It is important to have high standards. For the most part, life will pay any price you ask of it. The people who achieve the most in the world have incredibly high standards. It is like this with businesses as well. A piece of machinery, or a service, is great because standards have been followed.

You have personal values, beliefs and performance benchmarks. Your business also has these characteristics, and they are referred to as company standards. Think of standards as your business personality and vision, coupled with the rules you live and work by. Your small business standards will likely mirror your personal standards, and your customers, clients and employees will form an opinion about your business – and your brand – based on these values.

What are standards?

Your standards define how your company acts, which, in turn, builds trust in your brand. They can be guidelines that describe quality, performance, safety, terminology, testing, or management systems, to name a few. They can comply with authoritative agencies or professional organisations, and can be enforceable by law, such as doctors needing to have medical degrees, or financial planners needing to hold a CFP or CII certification. Or they can be voluntary rules you establish to create confidence among your clients that your business operates at a high and consistent quality level, such as a restaurant using only locally sourced ingredients of the highest quality.

Standards must align with your mission, business objectives, and organisational leadership, and be implemented consistently across your enterprise. Employees need to buy in to the value of adhering to standards so everyone is pulling in the same direction and reinforcing your brand.

Controlling and measuring standards

Standards are what your business aspires to, but they don't guarantee performance. You need to create processes to control how your standards are implemented, and measure and evaluate how they help your business grow. Written guidelines, technical specifications, product inspection processes, management and financial audits, and even customer surveys can be effective performance indicators and help you determine if you're meeting your standards, or if the standards need to be tweaked in some way.

The psychology of standards separates the best people from the ordinary. People with high standards believe that everything matters and that nothing is small enough not to have a benchmark or standard. They hold themselves to high standards because they know that without doing so, they will not get to where they want to go, or become the person they want to be. They get 'stressed' about not meeting the standards (their goals) and use this stress to drive themselves forward to get better and better. Stress becomes drive when you convert it. You want to have stress to drive yourself forward.

Working in an exceptional law firm is stressful precisely because it has such high standards. Everything is taken very seriously and the culture of the law firm is based on high standards. It is like this with medicine, finance and everywhere else where the people are the very best at what they do.

When you work with exceptional people, you'll notice that they generally have high standards, and these standards will rub off on you. You become like the people you spend time with. This is why people who come out of certain workplaces where high standards are rigorously enforced tend to do better in the job market. Potential new employers believe that they, too, will have high standards.

You can see how standards work in the fitness arena. If someone is a professional bodybuilder, they are generally going to be far more demanding of themselves from a fitness standpoint than someone who is not. They are going to work out harder, lift more, eat differently and live a different lifestyle from someone without those standards.

The importance of being extraordinary

When law firms, companies and others lay people off, the people who lose their jobs are generally the people who are 'good'. People who are 'outstanding' don't lose their jobs (or hardly ever). Outstanding people are the ones who bring hard work, constant improvement and greatness to whatever they do. The world needs people who are outstanding and who set the highest goals possible for themselves.

Everyone can be outstanding with the right standards. If you say you cannot be outstanding, you are slapping the face of your creator. There is nothing on this earth that does not have a purpose. You are in control over what happens to you and can control it by the standards you set for yourself. Life has meaning when you give it your all.

The secret lies in the standards you set for yourself and the decisions you make. What standards are you going to choose for your life?

Comfort in where you are is dangerous. People who get too comfortable are the ones who get fat, lose their jobs, whose spouses walk out on them and who die early deaths because they do not take good care of themselves. People who get too comfortable do not earn the respect of the world, their children, peers and others at anywhere near the level they are capable of. People who get too comfortable slowly waste away.

So how do companies with high standards get that way, and how do they maintain them? Well, high standards start at the top. Leadership sets those standards and communicates expectations to key people, who then communicate them throughout the organisation, no matter whether the whole organisation consists of one person or hundreds. They train people to the standards, create metrics, and review procedures to ensure the standards are maintained and enforced. If they find standards are not being maintained, they take remedial action. I know this sounds simple, but it really is not, and involves tremendous work and energy; no one said maintaining excellence was easy. It takes constant effort, year in and year out. But the benefits are enormous.

In general, businesses with high standards enjoy higher customer satisfaction and greater customer loyalty, lower levels of staff turnover and a happier workforce, better reputations and more referrals, and higher profit margins, which allows for greater investment in growth, because customers are, typically, willing to pay a little more to get the results and benefits of those higher standards. The result is a more sustainable, more profitable, and more enjoyable business for all concerned.

Assuming leadership is able to create and articulate those higher standards, it has to be realised this is not a 'snap-the-fingers-and-it-happens' project. It takes patience, fortitude and gumption to set higher standards and achieve them – but when it works, amazing things will happen.

CHAPTER THREE

Are we really understanding our customers or ignoring the facts?

'The single biggest problem in communication is the illusion that it has taken place'
– playwright George Bernard Shaw

In my 27-plus years in business and the entrepreneurial community, I have observed the success of many businesses, and the fast failure of others. All these companies had superior products or services – so why did some fail?

In the world of big data, business people face a dilemma. Sure, they have informationon customers. This information is piling up, because, for the most part, business owners are desperate not to miss any opportunity to record every touch point customers have with the company.

But then what? Now comes the entrepreneurial opportunity of the next five years. Turn your understanding of your customers into opportunities for real, meaningful connections with them. Listen to what they are really saying: not just their responses to surveys, but what they tell you when they do business with your company.

Your most precious asset, no matter what business you have, is your existing customers. You expended considerable effort to entice these companies to do business with you. So why not intensely focus on their behaviour as they do business with you?

Rather than comb through the endless data about them, talk to them – humanise your approach.

Too many companies squander the treasure that is real customer feedback. The solution is systematically measuring the customer's human voice and integrating it into a culture of continuous feedback.

Customer experience metrics have proliferated over the past decade, and chances are that your business relies heavily on one or more of them. But many companies struggle with metrics. For some, the problem is a disconnect between the metric and business performance; for others, it's a loss of confidence among frontline workers when the metrics do not seem to explain big swings in customer satisfaction. Further, in some companies, there is confusion about whether transactional or relational measures matter more, and, in others, a simple lack of results from too much focus on one top-line metric.

Loyal customers may represent no more than 20 per cent of your customer base, but make up more that 50 per cent of your sales. You need to be communicating with these customers on a regular basis. These people are the ones who can and should influence your marketing decisions. Nothing will make a loyal customer feel better than soliciting their input and showing them how much you value it. Still, you need to consider that not all regular customers are loyal to your company. You need to be able to classify your customers and identify the loyal ones correctly if you plan to make marketing decisions based on their interests.

Taken together, these complications leave many companies tone-deaf to the voice of the customer and represent a formidable barrier to building the foundation of a successful customer-centric strategy. Happily, our experience shows that it matters less which top-line metric a business relies on; almost any one will do. Rather, what matters is how the business inserts the metric into a systematic capability to collect, analyse, and act on feedback in an effective and complete measurement system of the customer journey.

Building that system can take time, but gains to a customer-centric culture and the bottom line can accrue quickly.

Customers have choices when buying a product. They seek options from trusted friends and family. Experienced shoppers explore what others are saying on social media and online customer reviews. Your company's product may be one of many options. You can benefit from listening to your customers' opinions about their level of satisfaction with competing products. Take the time to thoroughly explore what others are saying about your competition. What you hear might provide you with information critical to helping you deliver better solutions.

All great and successful company leaders have a clear understanding of their customers. It is the basis of why a company exists. It's the foundation of an organisation's vision and strategy. You could have an exceptional product, but if you fail to consider how it fits the needs of your buyer, you don't have a business. We need to learn what our current and future customers need, and make sure we deliver exactly what they want for a price they will pay. Customers, if we listen to them, will tell us all we need to know to develop the right products and services to grow a viable business. Great businesses, large and small, follow this model today. They talk to customers constantly, always taking note of any changes in thought or behaviour.

CHAPTER FOUR

Why are our human-to-human relationships so disconnected from real life?

'Social media websites are no longer performing an envisaged function of creating a positive communication link among friends, family and professionals. It is a veritable battle-ground, where insults fly from the human quiver, damaging lives, destroying self-esteem and a person's sense of self-worth'

– international judge Anthony Carmona

For a long time, I've been interested in what I term 'the cruel world of human-to-human relationships'. A very good friend and colleague recently reinforced the subject when he said: "Can you please tell me why we do not trust one another to speak human to human today? Why are people so crazy for email, WhatsApp, Twitter, Facebook, YouTube, LinkedIn? Yes, these are all new and wonderful ways we can now connect with one another electronically, each with its own culture and unique set of rules, and, in one sense, the planet has never been more interconnected. And yet this overly interconnected world, while wonderful, also seems to come with a cost to human-to-human relationships."

I pondered and then smiled, telling him, "If you look around you on your daily commute, or even while you're walking down the street, you will observe people reaching out for their smartphone as soon as there's an alert, and they'll be checking email and responding to texts and social media channels. Brain scans have shown that dopamine, the pleasure neurotransmitter, is released every time we hear our phone beep. This means we can become addicted to using our phones to a certain extent and it can be tough to break the habit. You may need to put in place something to reinforce the change in behaviour until it becomes second nature. The rest of the day, people are constantly on a tablet, mobile device, laptop or desktop for personal or professional use. The whole world is messaging, browsing, friending, tweeting and sharing."

It's great that we have the technology to connect with people across the globe instantly, but there is also a sense of disconnection. If there's an internet-capable device with a screen anywhere nearby, the immediate world does not get our full attention.

Much has been written about the dangers of internet addiction. From watching sport to merely surfing the web, the internet is clearly the television of the 21st century, an electronic drug that often yanks us away from the physical world. Like any addiction, the real cost, for those of us who are truly addicted, is to the number and quality of our relationships with others. We may enjoy online relationships using social media sites like Facebook or Twitter, for example, but the difference between these kinds of interactions and engaging with people in the physical world is vast. As long as we expect no more from these online relationships than they can give, no good reason exists why we cannot enjoy the power of social media to connect us efficiently to people we would otherwise not be able to reach. The problem, however, comes when we find ourselves subtly substituting electronic relationships for physical ones, or mistaking our electronic relationships for physical ones. We may feel we're connecting effectively with others via the internet, but too much electronic-relating paradoxically engenders a sense of social isolation.

I cannot tell you how many times I have wondered what someone did really mean by their words, whether on social media, in a text or over email. Unless you see the person's face, hear their voice and understand the environment, you have no idea about the context surrounding the written words. Misunderstandings, miscommunication, wrongful interpretations and assumptions result, which have an impact on how we view others.

Online contact falls short on empathy. As a corollary to the context issue, there's an utter lack of empathy when using technology to interact with others. Take, for example, 'I'm so sorry you feel this way', or 'I heard you lost your job; I feel for you'. Where is the compassion and solidarity with loss? It certainly does exist within the soul of the person who texted, posted or emailed, but words alone do not convey it.

Technology fails to deliver the essential personal touch. Tech overload leads to an increase in stress and psychological issues: technology has become an electronic addiction for some, taking them out of the physical world as they cling to the features it offers. Like many addictions, there's an impact on the number and quality of human relationships. Conversations through social media and email take the place of traditional interactions and discussions; eventually, a person doesn't even need to leave the house to communicate with others – and many people won't. The phenomenon leads to social isolation that can be crippling for some.

For transferring information efficiently, the internet is excellent. For transacting emotionally sensitive or satisfying connections, it is absolutely not. Even when we are all careful to use the internet only to exchange information, problems can still arise. People tend to delay answering emails, or block and ignore calls when the email or call doesn't contain what they consider to be good answers, or when they want to avoid whatever responsibility is being demanded of them. This is like being asked a question in person, and rather than responding, 'I don't know' or 'I'll have to think about it', turning on your heels and walking away in silence. It is far easier to ignore an email sender's request than a request from someone made in person, because an email sender's hope of getting a response (or frustration in not receiving one) remains mostly invisible. But it's every bit as rude.

Institute for Fiscal Studies research sampled 143 married or cohabiting women. Each woman reported how often certain devices, such as smartphones, tablets, computers and TVs, interrupted the interactions she had with her spouse or partner. The women also rated how often specific technology interruption situations occurred, such as a partner sending text messages to others during the couple's face-to-face conversations or being on their phone during mealtimes.

Overall, about 70 per cent of the women in the sample said that smartphones, computers, or TV interfered in their relationship with their partner at least sometimes or more often.

Many women also said that the following specific interruptions happened at least daily:

- 62 per cent said technology interfered with their leisure time together

- 40 per cent said their partner got distracted by the TV during a conversation

- 35 per cent said their partner would pull out their phone if they received a notification, even if the couple were in the middle of a conversation

- 33 per cent said their partner checked their phone during mealtimes they spenttogether

- 25 per cent said their partner actively texted other people during the couple's face-to-face conversations.

Technology has become an integral part of our lives, with more and more of us emailing, texting, tweeting and facebooking. A recent survey by Facebook found the first thing 80 per cent of people did in the mornings was check their phones. The average user then went on to check their device 110 times a day.

You would think that this must mean that we are more connected to each other than ever – but what exactly does it mean for romantic relationships? Are we giving our partners the time and attention they need? Or are we spending more time than we should in our own worlds with our always-on technology?

Research conducted by Princeton Survey Research Associates

International on a sample of 2,252 Americans last year indicated cause for worry: 25 per cent felt their partner was distracted by their phone when they were together, and 8 per cent had argued as a result.

The figures were worse for younger people: 42 per cent of 18-to-29-year-olds said their partners had been distracted by their phones, and 18 per cent had argued over the amount of time the other was spending online.

Our 'emotional invisibility' on the internet perhaps also explains so much of the vitriol we see on so many websites. People clearly have a penchant for saying things in the electronic world that they'd never say to people in person, because the person to whom they're saying it isn't physically present to display their emotional reaction. It's as if the part of our nervous system that registers the feelings of others has been paralysed or removed when we're communicating electronically, as if we're drunk and don't realise or don't care that our words are hurting others.

Social media websites are wonderful tools but are often abused. A few common sense rules for the electronic world apply:

- Do not say anything on email you would feel uncomfortable saying to someone in person

- Do not delay your response to messages you would rather avoid

- Relationships are affected by online communication

- Balance time on the internet with time well spent with friends, family and outside interests.

What we all need to remember is that real world relationships are absolutely vital to our mental health. Technology has given us the ability to stay constantly connected, constantly at work, but it's not technology's fault. Let's instead look in the mirror and realise who's really to blame here. It's time to take control of our technology and our lives so that we can rediscover the wonderful treasures that are buried in those separate realities we once had. Remember, there's a time to plug in and a time to unplug. Choose wisely.

All in all, trust is a huge issue with online presence and the impact of technology on human interaction paints a pretty gloomy picture. But it is a valuable discussion to have, as it teaches us the value of balancing our offline and online communications with others, personally and professionally. I guess the best approach is to make yourself available through technology only when appropriate, so that it supplements relationships rather than replacing them.

CHAPTER FIVE

More management, more leaders – or are we failing in business?

'Technology is a compulsive and addictive way to live. Verbal communication cannot be lost because of a lack of skill. The ability to listen and learn is key to mastering the art of communication. If you don't use your verbal skills and networking, it will disappear rapidly. Use technology wisely'
– basketball coach Rick Pitino

I have always maintained that you cannot train a leader; leadership is in your DNA or not, and I believe that leadership is something in your blood. The route of success in any business is with the strength of its leadership, so the question that I am always engaging with in these days is why is there so much management, why do we have a shortage of competent and strong leaders?

Others share my views on leadership. If you read chapter seven of John Bogle's book *Enough: True Measures of Money, Business and Life*, you'll see that the theme of management versus leadership is a familiar one, and the distinctions that Bogle makes are based on some fairly standard and familiar definitions. To clarify the distinguishing features, Bogle quotes Professor Bennis as follows:

The manager administers, the leader innovates, and the manager relies on control; the leader inspires trust; the manager has a short-range view; the leader has a long-range perspective; the manager accepts the status quo, the leader challenges it.

The need for leadership is as strong if not stronger in IT as it is in the worlds of finance and business with which Bogle is primarily concerned.

Calls have been made consistently over a long period of time now by a large number of business gurus, life coaches and consultants, but still the landscape remains patchy.

For every good piece of leadership I see, where teams are given clear direction and empowered to operate effectively, I see examples of micro-management where managers are insistent on predetermining the activities, tasks and man-day estimates and then badgering the team to report their success in following this predetermined plan.

A great leader will possess qualities like passion, integrity, a 'take charge' attitude and the ability to inspire others. Employers and executives recognise this, and these 'born leaders' are often first in line for promotions to leadership roles.

Yet people with leadership potential have never become leaders overnight. Existing leaders have a responsibility to train the next generation, showing them how to guide a group of people towards a specific vision or goal, which in this new digital era of automation, robot and in some exception non-verbal communication is a particularly difficult challenge to overcome.

We live in a world where never before has leadership been so necessary but where so often leaders seem to come up short. Our sense is that this is not really a problem of individuals; this is a problem of organisational structures, effectively those traditional pyramidal structures that demand too much of too few and not enough of everyone else. Here we are in a world of complex organisations that require too much from those few people at the top. They do not always have the intellectual diversity, the bandwidth, the time to really make all these critical decisions. There is always a reason that, so often in organisations, change is belated, infrequent and convulsive.

The dilemma is due to complex company organisation, coupled with growth – as fast as the environment is changing, there are not enough extraordinary leaders to go around (this is something that I majored on in *Meaningful Conversations*). Look at what we expect from a leader today. We expect somebody to be confident and yet humble. We expect them to be very strong in themselves but open to being influenced. We expect them to be amazingly prescient but to be practical as well, to be extremely bold and also prudent.

So, can organisations develop real leaders that can make a difference to business and create value?

My belief is that emotional intelligence is going to be a huge key component of effective and developed leadership. The ability to be perceptively in tune with yourself and your emotions, as well as having sound situational awareness, can be a powerful tool for leading a team. The act of knowing, understanding, and responding to emotions, overcoming stress in the moment, and being aware of how your words and actions affect others, is fundamental for growth. Emotional intelligence for leadership consists of five attributes: self-awareness, self-management, empathy, relationship management, and effective communication.

The business world is evolving and changing at unprecedented speed in an unconnected human world, and emotions and our day-to-day communications are becoming more important in working relationships. Having emotional intelligence increases your chances of being accepted onto teams and considered for leadership positions. It can also set you apart from the competition when seeking a new position or promotion.

Sharing information is critical, but it is substantially less than half the battle. You must communicate clearly about the organisation's strategy, speed, direction, and results. But you cannot stop there. Verbally and nonverbally, the way in which you communicate – humbly, passionately, confidently – has more impact than the words you choose.

As a leader, you must inspire others through your words and actions. And before you speak, make sure you listen and observe; knowing your audience is as important as the message you're delivering. Communication informs, persuades, guides, and assures, as well as inspires. You must be willing to reveal more of yourself, to let others see your soul. If you withdraw, you will undermine your effectiveness as a leader, and your followers may soon drift to the side lines.

In summary, clear communication is the most important key to a business leader's success. So, to grow as a leader and manager, you must learn how to be an effective, compelling communicator. And if you want your company to succeed, you and your team have to master the art of clear communication together, as well. By using these and other strategies, you and your employees can reach new levels of leadership excellence.

CHAPTER SIX

How can a meaningful conversation help your business?

'Choose to focus your time, energy and conversation around people who inspire you, support you and help you to grow you into your happiest, strongest, wisest self'
– author and designer Karen Salmansohn

Conversations are key in language development, in the exchange of thoughts and ideas, and in listening to each other. People learn by hearing each other's thoughts while observing facial and body expressions that show emotions.

"Face-to-face conversation is the most human and humanising thing we do," says Sherry Turkle in her book *Reclaiming Conversation – The Power of Talk in a Digital Age.*

"Fully present to one another, we learn to listen. It is where we develop the capacity for empathy. It's where we experience the joy of being heard and of being understood. Conversation advances self-reflection, the conversations with ourselves that are the cornerstone of early development and continue throughout life."

Technology is a part of everyday life, but replacing face-to-face conversation with phone conversation, via texting, emailing, etc, has taken important skills away from children and young adults.

In today's world, there is a "flight from conversation", as Turkle says. All ages of people cannot do without phones and screens, but a balance is of utmost importance. How much time do you typically spend with others? And when you do, how connected and at tuned to them do you feel? Your answers to these simple questions may well reveal your biological capacity to connect.

If you've ever been trapped in an lift with a casual acquaintance, you know just how painful small talk can be. 'What a shame we're stuck in the office on such a beautiful day', or 'How was your weekend?' There might be a smile accompanying this, but the other person is not speaking because they care about the quality of your weekend; it's because there's an awkward silence that begs to be filled.

There's a reason small talk like this exists. If your fellow lift rider were to ask you about your darkest secrets or deepest wishes while the two of you descended floors in a tiny metal box, you would probably feel that that was too much intimacy, too early on in your relationship.

Yet small talk can help you probe for more interesting topics to talk about. For example, if you were to answer by saying, 'My weekend was great! I bought the final component for my laser defence drone,' your lift companion would definitely have some follow-up questions*.

The instant and omnipresent realm of communication has increased our capacity to connect on a perfunctory level, but in some cases has thwarted our capacity to have real and meaningful face-to-face conversations. The two forms of communication

– virtual and physical – can work in tandem, and although the physical kind obviously takes a bit more effort, it most often results in a far more meaningful experience.

A popular article in *The New York Times*, "Your phone vs your heart", mirrored some of these observations. In particular, the article explored how we can 're-wire' our hearts and brains to become more undisturbed. The article contends, "If you don't regularly exercise your ability to connect face to face, you'll eventually find yourself lacking some of the basic biological capacity to do so." To summarise the piece, it warns that if you don't go out of your way to form meaningful, personal friendships beyond the virtual ones, you may lose the ability to do so in the future. A sort of 'use it or lose it' model.

What was also intriguing about the article was that it said that through these face-to-face connections, you actually build up your biological capacity to not only empathise but also improve your health.

Heidegger in 1966 probably had it right when he made the prescient statement, "Technology makes us at home everywhere and nowhere [at the same time]."

We are more connected than ever, yet we remain walled off behind our smartphones, mobile devices and computer screens. Perhaps our communication tools are more cosmetic than we think; they have yet to master the ancient and inimitable art of human contact.

Your success is determined in large part by your ability to have a conversation. You can be the best at what you do, but if you're not communicating effectively with clients, staff and the market, then you're missing opportunities. There are many different ways to look at communication in the small business world, from writing and speaking as an individual to client communication and employee management in a company-wide context.

Each and every day you will be required to flex your communication muscles and interact; a bad conversation could spell disaster for an employee relationship, a customer or your business. Alternatively, the right words at the right time could propel your business to places you didn't think possible and deliver opportunities that were not available before. We should all stay inspired with ideas and innovation, creating great things!

★   Interestingly, meaningful conversations are not restricted to, or guaranteed by, long-term relationships. I've had deeper conversations with strangers on an aeroplane than with some people I've known for decades.

CHAPTER SEVEN

Purposeful driven discussions with Mark Herbert

*'When you're surrounded by people who share a
passionate commitment around a common purpose,
anything is possible'*
– businessman and billionaire Howard Schultz

Every year, I travel to Oregon to visit my business partner, Mark Herbert, to discuss cross-border challenges and to hold meetings with his team. My relationship with Mark and his team is a good example of a 'special relationship' that has grown from strength to strength over the last decade. We always discuss US and Europe and the effects on business of the personnel who hold office, as well as the challenges of working in an increasingly fast-paced and ever-changing world.

On my last visit, Mark and I decided to take a road trip to the beautiful town of Brownsville. Originally known as Calapooya, after the area's original inhabitants, the Kalapuya Indians, or 'Kirk's Ferry', after the ferry operated across the Calapooia River by early settlers Alexander and Sarah Kirk, Brownsville was the location of filming for the1985 film Stand by Me, directed by Rob Reiner.

As we drove the back roads in Mark's Porsche convertible, I started to ask him about purpose-driven outcomes in business.

"Great subject, Geoff," he said. "You could question whether wondering too openly, or intensely, about the meaning of life sounds like a peculiar, ill-fated and unintentionally comedic pastime. It isn't anything an ordinary mortal should be doing – or would get very far by doing. A select few might be equipped to take on the task and discover the answer in their own lives, but such ambition isn't for most of us. Meaningful lives are for extraordinary people: great saints, artists, scholars, scientists, doctors, activists, explorers, national leaders. If ever we did discover the meaning, it would – we suspect – in any case be incomprehensible, perhaps written in Latin or in computer code. It wouldn't be anything that could orient or illuminate our activities. Without always acknowledging it, we are – in the background – operating with a remarkably ungenerous perspective on the meaning of life."

I responded with, "It is my belief that an important part of empathy is the ability to trust and be trusted. When your employees feel that you care, then you have earned their trust. If they trust you, they will take more risks with you and be more open with you. People will talk openly with you only when they trust you. As trust builds, there will be more sharing of information, feelings, and thoughts. The more you share, the easier it is to relate to one another. Building trust is something that takes time and effort. It involves both you and the other person in the relationship. The level of trust is what makes each relationship unique."

So how do you build a trusting relationship with someone? Mark listed five ways to build trusting relationships: learn to trust others; earn the trust of others; share information, thoughts and feelings; show weakness and take risks; be personable.

And he's right. If you want to develop your organisation's culture around purpose, it's hard to imagine anything more critical to your success than trust. Yet, unfortunately, trust is sorely lacking in workplaces in the US and Europe, in fact across the globe, reflecting society's growing distrust of business, government and other vital institutions.

How big is the trust gap? I recently read The 2017 Edelman Trust Barometer, which recently found that 37 per cent of respondents found CEOs to be credible spokespeople, down 12 per cent compared to 2016. Trust in employees is also falling. Edelman found that 48 per cent of respondents found employees trustworthy, down from 52 per cent in 2016. In fact, for the first time, a majority of global respondents said that they no longer trusted 'the system' – government, media, business and institutions – to work for them.

It's clear there's a crisis of trust brewing. Yet, there's hope for companies that pursue purpose transformation, for it is only by being trustworthy that we can gain the trust of employees, customers and others who are invested in mutual success.

Mark went on to say that "organisations' values play another vital role". "Values prevent teams and individuals from giving into that short term, numbers-oriented mentality that is so prevalent in many publicly traded organisations," he said. "We have to give up the notion that it's okay for work to be unsatisfying; that it's simply an obligation versus something we feel fulfilled and passionate about doing. We as individuals have to change our beliefs; that's what really changes the organisation."

The ability to trust your team to embody your values is the foundation for a successful purpose transformation. After all, you can expend a lot of energy defining purpose and values, but if you can't rely on your team to embody them, then it won't impact how teams interact with customers and each other, and it won't impact how business gets done.

Values should drive decision-making, especially around hiring and retention. Organisations must hire people who believe in the organisation's purpose, and who embody the values you want to see in your organisation.

I continued to question Mark, asking him, "So how do you build a trust-based workplace?"

His response made clear that inspiring trust is about walking the walk and great storytelling. "As a leader, you build trust by making yourself available and listening to questions. You have to listen to your customers and your people, and recognise the questions people have."

It might not seem like trust is a crucial component of building a purpose-driven organisation. But in truth, it's trust – between employees and managers, managers and executive leaders, and customers and those within the organisation – that gives purpose and values the power to transform.

To be successful in today's dynamic business environment, leaders must work toward building relevance, managing business fundamentals with a balanced approach, and guiding employees through open, two-way communication. Those leaders that leverage opportunities to adapt, innovate and learn can make ever-changing times invigorating and advantageous for themselves, their employees and their organisations.

CHAPTER EIGHT

The tide is rising on the fourth industrial revolution

The changes are so profound that, from the perspective of human history, there has never been a time of greater promise or potential peril.

– executive chairman of the World Economic Forum, Klaus Schwab

Many experts now believe that a person's emotional intelligence quotient (EQ) may be more important than their IQ, and it is certainly a better predictor of success, quality of relationships, meaningful conversations and overall happiness.

Emotion has long been something of a taboo subject in the workplace. It's widely seen as inherently negative – it clouds decision-making, allegedly it's a source of weakness, and should not be shown at the office. But recent changes in business and the wider world have caused a seismic shift in how people view emotion and appreciate its power when used intelligently.

One of the root causes of this shift is that the composition of the workforce has changed vastly over a relatively short period. It has become far more diverse in terms of ethnicity, culture, religion, gender and sexuality. And a gap has opened up, especially between members of the older generations, who run most organisations, and the millennials and Gen Z-ers who work for them when it comes to personal values and expectations of employment.

The Deloitte Global Millennial Survey 2019 found that millennials (defined by the researchers as those born between January 1983 and December 1994) and Gen Z-ers (born January 1995 to December 1999) are mistrustful of businesses that prioritise their own agenda over their impact on society. Many respondents to the Deloitte Global Millennial Survey said they would cut immediate ties with any company that didn't share their values.

The fourth industrial revolution is the current and developing environment in which disruptive technologies and trends such as the Internet of Things (IoT), robotics, virtual reality (VR) and artificial intelligence (AI) are changing the way we live and work. We're looking at not just technological assistance, but a flourishing form of technological assimilation.

The World Economic Forum now considers EQ a crucial skill for the fourth industrial revolution, while research has always shown that EQ improves decision-making and morale in organisations.

Move over, IQ; it's not just about increased academia any more. The fourth industrial revolution will change how we interact with one another in conjunction with our technology, and it requires that we reconnect with our EQ. Artificial intelligence (AI) is increasingly making its way into the decision-making processes of modern business, yet emotional and social intelligence remain two capabilities that can't be automated yet.

In fewer than five years, more than a third (35 per cent) of skills considered important today will have changed, according to a report by the World Economic Forum. Among cognitive abilities such as complex problem solving and critical thinking, emotional intelligence – often referred to as 'street smarts' – has been identified as a crucial social skill that will be needed by all.

The report, based on the opinions of chief HR and strategy officers from leading global organisations, suggests that seismic advances in technology, including AI, advanced robotics and machine learning, will revolutionise the way we live and work. As a result, organisations and employees will be under growing pressure to upgrade and fine tune their skillsets to thrive, or even survive, this fourth industrial revolution.

It's one thing to have complex thinkers with lightning-fast computational skills and incomparable technical abilities, but it's quite another to have an intercommunicative workforce that's situationally aware and adaptive. Consider the example of FedEx, which took EQ to heart when designing its leadership programme. By focusing on building emotional intelligence into its management team, the company has yielded an 8-11 per cent increase in core leadership competencies. Employees also made vast improvements in their decision-making and influencing abilities and experienced a marked improvement in their quality of life.

According to the World Economic Forum report, dated 21 January 2019, by 2020 there will be a greater bidding war for employees with social abilities including persuasion and emotional intelligence compared to more limited technical skills like programming or equipment operation and control.

Furthermore, professions previously seen as purely technical will see a new demand for interpersonal skills, such as being able to communicate data effectively. Emotional intelligence is likely to be a major deciding factor in who will be able to adapt and flourish in these new roles.

In his books, *Emotional Intelligence: Why it can Matter More Than IQ* and *Workingwith Emotional Intelligence*, Daniel Goleman presents five categories of emotional intelligence.

To hire candidates that will thrive in your workplace, look for those who have a handle on these five pillars:

1. Self-awareness: If a person has a healthy sense of self-awareness, they understand their own strengths and weaknesses, as well as how their actions affect others. A person who is self-aware is usually better able to handle and learn from constructive criticism than one who is not

2. Self-regulation: A person with a high EQ can maturely reveal their emotions and exercise restraint when needed. Instead of squelching their feelings, they express them with restraint and control

3. Motivation: Emotionally intelligent people are self-motivated. They're not motivated simply by money or a title. They are usually resilient and optimistic when they encounter disappointment and are driven by an inner ambition

4. Empathy: A person who has empathy has compassion and an understanding of human nature that allows them to connect with other people on an emotional level. The ability to empathise allows a person to provide great service and respond genuinely to others' concerns

5. People skills: People who are emotionally intelligent are able to build rapport and trust quickly with others on their teams. They avoid power struggles and backstabbing. They usually enjoy other people and have the respect of others around them.

Effective leadership requires mastering and blending both left- and right-brain thinking.

Accenture recently conducted a research study across 200 C-suite executives from France, Germany, Italy, Spain, the UK and the US, which indicated that to push the C-suite to find new ways to lead, grow and sustain their organisations demanded a new type of leader to engage passion, principles and capabilities. The expectation? Leaders who have a strong balance across analytics-led and human-centred skills.

This approach blends what has traditionally been considered 'left-brain' (scientific) skills that draw on data analysis and critical reasoning with 'right-brain' (creative) skills that draw on areas like intuition and empathy. Bringing the two together intentionally to drive deeper levels of problem solving and value creation is critical.

But the majority (89 per cent) of today's C-suite leaders hold business school, science, or technology degrees and have honed 'left brain' skills such as critical reasoning, decision-making and results-orientation. Numbers. Data. Stats. The science of management, rooted in reasoning and proof points. This has served them well, and these capabilities will always be vital. But they are no longer sufficient.

As the pace of change continues to accelerate and we head towards the fourth industrial revolution, being able to identify and anticipate future skills requirements will be crucial. The organisations and employees that embrace and prepare for the changes will be the biggest winners.

Look around you: tech is being transfused into the veins of every industry. You need to make an educated guess as to how – and which – new technologies could impact your business and then act.

Rapid disruptive change is inevitable, and the assimilation of technology into every aspect of modern business is unavoidable. The question is whether today's business leaders can remain competitive in a technological world that's rapidly and exponentially evolving.

PART TWO

Strategy

CHAPTER NINE

So exactly how do we value time?

'The most exciting, challenging and significant relationship of all is the one you have with yourself. And if you can find someone to love the you [that] you love... well, that's just fabulous'
– actress Sarah Jessica Parker

I recently had breakfast with a senior partner of an exceptional accounting firm in London. He is a personal friend and associate and we often meet to discuss many strategic topics. During breakfast we decided to focus on one of his questions: "What is the most valuable commodity we all have today?" The answer I gave was "time".

But what exactly is time and how do we qualify it?

According to Wikipedia, time is the indefinite continued progress of existence and events that occur in apparently irreversible succession from the past through the present to the future. Time is a component quantity of various measurements used to sequence events, to compare the duration of events or the intervals between them, and to quantify rates of change of quantities in material reality or in the conscious experience.

Time is often referred to as the fourth dimension, along with the three spatial dimensions.

As time is something none of us can get more of, managing it well is one of the most important things you can do as a purposeful leader.

One of the best analogies you can use in your company regarding time is asking your employees to equate one hour of time to one pound. When I was in corporate management, I would ask directors who came through my door: "Is that a £1 decision? A £100 pound decision? Or a £1,000 decision?"

If they gave the third answer, I allowed them to take a seat.

It really is helpful to look at your time just as you look at investing your money. Because, in essence, you are looking for the same result: you are looking for the best return.

Taking this thought process one step further, ask yourself, "Who am I spending my time with?" All too often, managers spend their time where the problems are, not where the results are. While we need to deal with problems, we want our focus to be on results. Our job as leaders puts us in a position where we have to deal with problems and poor performance. But we need some parameters to help us understand both the issue of time and the investment of time.

One of the most touted management/leadership teachings out there is: 'Spend 80 per cent of your time with your top performers.' Another is: 'Your team should be measured based on the 20 per cent top performers, 70 per cent role players and 10 per cent poor performers.' In theory, I agree. But I think these teachings fall short. Not enough is written, or taught, about the critical 80 per cent of your workforce and how to improve their performance through minimum performance standards.

Time is seen differently by Eastern and Western cultures, and even from country to country. In the Western hemisphere, the US and Mexico employ time in such opposing manners that it causes intense friction between the two peoples. As an example, everyone in Mexico knows the name of the president of the United States. You should know the name of Mexico's current president and have some clue about the country's history and current challenges.

In Western Europe, the Swiss attitude to time bears little relation to that of neighbouring Italy. This seems like common sense, but in a country with four official languages it can admittedly be daunting. This is in fact one of the common gripes that the Swiss have against foreigners. English is understood almost everywhere but a little bonjour, ciao or hallo goes a long way to ingratiating yourself with the locals.

Thai people do not evaluate the passing of time in the same way that the Japanese do. In the UK the future stretches out in front of you; in Madagascar, people believe it flows into the back of your head from behind.

Let us begin with the American concept of time, for theirs is the most expensive, as anyone who has had to deal with American doctors, dentists or lawyers will tell you.

For an American, time is truly money. In a profit-oriented society, time is a precious, even scarce, commodity. It flows fast, like a mountain river in the spring, and if you want to benefit from its passing, you have to move fast with it. Americans are people of action; they cannot bear to be idle. The past is over, but the present you can seize, parcel and package and make it work for you in the immediate future. In the US you have to make money, otherwise you are nobody. If you have 40 years of earning capacity and you want to make $4million, that means $100,000 per annum. If you can achieve this in 250 working days a year, that comes to $400 a day, or $50 an hour. So Americans can say that their time costs $50 an hour. Americans also talk about wasting, spending, budgeting and saving time.

This seems logical enough, until one begins to apply the idea to other cultures. Has the Portuguese fisherman, who failed to hook a fish in two hours, wasted his time? Has the Sicilian priest, failing to make a convert on Thursday, lost ground? Have the German composer, the French poet, the Spanish painter, devoid of ideas last week, missed opportunities that can be qualified in monetary terms?

The Americans are not the only ones who sanctify timekeeping, for it is practically a religion in Switzerland and Germany, too. These countries, along with Britain and the Anglo-Saxon world in general, the Netherlands, Austria and Scandinavia, have a linear vision of time and action. They suspect, like the Americans, that time is passing (being wasted) without decisions being made or actions being performed.

These groups are also monochronic; that is, they prefer to do only one thing at a time, to concentrate on it and do it within a fixed schedule. They think that in this way they get more things done – and more efficiency. Furthermore, being imbued with a Protestant work ethic, they equate working time with success: the harder you work – the more hours, that is – the more successful you will be and the more money you will make.

Richard Lewis, who wrote *When Cultures Collide*, has a view that in countries inhabited by linear-active people, time is clock- and calendar-related, segmented in an abstract manner for our convenience, measurement, and disposal. In multiactive cultures like the Arab and Latin spheres, time is event- or personality-related, a subjective commodity which can be manipulated, moulded, stretched, or dispensed with, irrespective of what the clock says.

"I have to rush," says the American, "my time is up." The Spaniard or Arab, scornful of this submissive attitude to schedules, would only use this expression if death were imminent.

In a Buddhist culture, such as in Thailand or Tibet, not only time but also life itself goes around in a circle. Whatever we plan, however we organise our particular world, generation follows generation; governments and rulers will succeed each other; crops will be harvested; monsoons, earthquakes and other catastrophes will recur; taxes will be paid; the sun and moon will rise and set; stocks and shares will rise and fall. Even the Americans will not change such events, certainly not by rushing things.

Cyclic time is not seen as a straight road leading from our feet to the horizon, but as a curved one which in one year's time will lead us through 'scenery' and conditions very similar to what we experience at the present moment. Observers of cyclic time are less disciplined in their planning of the future, since they believe that it cannot be managed and that humans make life easier for themselves by 'harmonising' with the laws and cyclic events of nature. Yet in such cultures a general form of planning is still possible, for many things are fairly regular and well understood.

As a business leader, you must understand the value of making a time management decision on where to spend your time to get the most beneficial results for your company. Your top 20 per cent will always perform at a high level, but you do need to devote time to coaching them to even greater success. That's a very good use of 80 per cent of your time and effort.

The other 20 per cent of your time, focused on the remaining 80 per cent of your workforce or team, should be used to establish, communicate and promote the minimum standards for working at your company. The message you want to communicate is, "You have to work at a certain level if you want to work here". You must clearly establish that you no longer allow employees to come to work and just exist without being accountable to minimum standards.

If you adopt this concept, you will find that 80 per cent of your employee base willcontribute to the growth and success of your company or department, and your top 20 per cent performers will be inspired to try even harder. The point is, your top performers will always perform at a high level. You do need to invest your time with them to coach them to even greater success. Using the remaining 20 per cent of your time to raise the standards of the other 80 per cent of your employees will create an environment of incremental growth through your largest body of employees.

So, what is the conclusion around the true worth of time?

My belief is, know your value and do not accept being treated in a way less than you deserve. You must have realistic expectations, demands and a sense of entitlement. I am saying that as an individual you need to be treated the way you treat others, and vice versa. The minute you negotiate your self-worth and accept less, you say to the universe that you do not deserve any better, and the vicious cycle/patterns will start to begin. Change for yourself – and, of course, friends and partners are great mirror reflections that help you grow.

Time is not money. This adage has got us all into a lot more trouble than we realise. Because we live our lives based on the misleading premise that time is money, we attempt to do more in less time. We begin to confuse activity with productivity, as if the 'doing' will grant us 'being'. Inadvertently, we jump on the hamster wheel, running as fast as we can with a competitive mentality about the clock and what it supposedly represents in our lives and in the lives of others. We have a negative relationship with time that gives us a sense of time-starvation instead of abundance. Even our precious vacation time is not immune from the time/money equation.

CHAPTER TEN

Is customer loyalty sustainable in today's digital world?

'Companies and their brands need to reach out and speak directly to consumers, to honour their values, and to form meaningful relationships with them. They must become architects of community, consistently demonstrating the values that their customer community expects in exchange for their loyalty and purchases'

– leading brand consultant Simon Mainwaring

A good friend of mine in London operates a very successful marketing company. At lunch recently he asked me: "Do you think customers actually stay loyal to brands?"I replied that back in the early 2000s, we were all looking to deploy strategies across customer lifetime value. Customer lifetime value is one of the key stats likely to be tracked as part of a customer experience programme – brand satisfaction and lifetime value was a key part in our business survival toolbox. In today's world, customers who stay loyal to companies for long periods are rare.

The amount of trust consumers put in brands is decreasing all the time, and a typical consumer will now switch brands without hesitation if they get a better offer. The famous rule of 20 per cent of customers accounting for 80 per cent of turnover has turned into more like a 60/40 rule (40 per cent of the customers generate 60 per cent of turnover) and it is slowly evolving towards a 50/50 ratio, which will see both loyal and disloyal customers generating the same amount of income.

The conventional wisdom around competitive advantage is that successful companies pick a position, target a set of consumers, and configure activities to serve them better. The goal is to make customers repeat their purchases by matching the value proposition to their needs. By fending off competitors through ever-evolving uniqueness and personalisation, the company can achieve sustainable competitive advantage.

An assumption implicit in that definition is that consumers are making deliberate, perhaps even rational, decisions. Their reasons for buying products and services may be emotional, but they always result from somewhat conscious logic. Therefore a good strategy can figure out and respond to that logic.

But the idea that purchase decisions arise from conscious choice flies in the face of much research in behavioural psychology. The brain, it turns out, is not so much an analytical machine as a gap-filling machine: it takes noisy, incomplete information from the world and quickly fills in the missing pieces on the basis of past experience. Intuition, thoughts, opinions and preferences that come to mind quickly and without reflection, but which are strong enough to act on, are the products of this process.

This behavioural shift is putting some fundamental, established marketing tactics in doubt – but are we as marketers powerless to stop it?

Why customer loyalty is down

- Companies cannot keep up with rising consumer expectations

    Declining customer loyalty has been an issue for most companies in spite of heavy investments in service improvement. Consumers do not compare a company to where it was a year ago; rather, they compare companies to the 'best-in-class'. If Amazon does not question a faulty delivery and deals with the problem immediately, consumers will expect the same of their local supermarket

- Loyalty programmes are missing their mark

    Many companies thought there was a shortcut to creating customer loyalty: the loyalty card. However, all the latest studies agree that loyalty cards slash profit margins from existing customers. Instead of creating loyalty, you're losing money

- Digitisation makes everything transparent

    The fast adoption of smartphones and tablets has further enhanced transparency. Today, more than half of consumers use their mobile devices to compare prices while shopping. The online world has made price transparency very accessible – a trend that spells danger for any company out there

- Focusing on individual touch points instead of on the customer experience as a whole

Companies are divided into various departments, with every department being responsible for the customer's experience of a specific aspect of the customer relationship. For example, there is hardly any contact between the sales and after-sales departments, and invoicing is housed three floors down

- No unique relevance to consumers

    When customers are disloyal, what they are really saying is that a product or service was not relevant enough for them to remain a customer. Too little thought is put into the role a brand has to play in consumers' lives. The relationship is too rational in nature instead of emotional.

So what is the solution? According to popular theory, there are two ways to escape the commodity market. On the one hand a company can work more efficiently, making it possible to sell its products cheaper. On the other hand, you can offer a unique added value, thereby re-establishing differentiation, so you can charge higher prices again.

Historically, people engaged with brand loyalty – but how do you get customers to become loyal to your brand in the first place? Here are a few suggestions:

- Build targeted messages

    With social media being the centre of many people's lives, consumers want to see that brands care about them. Consumers are constantly bombarded with ads, so yours can easily get overlooked. How do you stand out? Try targeting your ads, using campaigns that appeal to your audience's interests, and customising your messages with a personal touch

• Develop a loyalty programme

Customer loyalty programmes are a huge factor in retaining loyal customers: 44 per cent of customers have two to four loyalty cards, and 25 per cent have between five and nine loyalty cards. In total, 43 per cent join loyalty programmes to earn rewards, and 45 per cent say it's a primary driver for purchasing from a brand. As you can see, loyalty programmes are a huge deal with customers, and it gets them to come back to your brand whenever they decide to shop.

However, be aware that you're more likely to retain customers through a free rewards programme. The majority of people (52 per cent) aren't willing to pay a membership fee

• Adopt a mobile strategy

Brand loyalty has gone mobile. A majority (77 per cent) of smartphone users say that mobile offers have a positive impact on their brand loyalty, according to accessdevelopment.com. This can include surprise points and rewards or exclusive content.

Another 66 per cent of consumers say they would have a more positive opinion of a loyalty programme if it was available on their smartphone or in a mobile wallet app. Furthermore, 73 per cent of smartphone users are interested in having loyalty cards on their phones.

What happens if you fall behind your competitors and don't offer a mobile solution to your loyalty programme? You'll likely see a decrease in customers. Two thirds of companies that saw a decrease in customer loyalty in the past year didn't have a mobile app.

- Implement feedback

   Another reason brands lose customers is because they don't respond to their needs. In today's fast-paced social landscape, customers expect brands to respond to their feedback – and quickly. Almost all (97 per cent) of customers surveyed by accessdevelopment.com say they are more likely to become loyal to a company that implements their feedback. By ignoring them, you are sending a message that their loyalty doesn't matter, and so they are likely to move on to a brand that shows them otherwise.

Although ideas about brand loyalty have shifted from generation to generation, people are still brand loyal today. However, you will have to adopt strong social and mobile strategies to retain customers who rely on the internet landscape to make buying decisions.

My opinion is that the subject of whether sustainable competitive advantage has disappeared is greatly exaggerated. Competitive advantage is as sustainable as it has always been. What is different today is that, in a world of infinite communication and innovation, many strategists seem convinced that sustainability can be delivered only by constantly making a company's value proposition the conscious consumer's rational or emotional first choice. They have forgotten, or they never understood, the dominance of the subconscious mind in decision-making. For fast thinkers, products and services that are easy to access and that reinforce comfortable buying habits will over time trump innovative but unfamiliar alternatives that may be harder to find and require forming new habits.

Essentially, customer lifetime value is the total worth to a business of a customer over the whole period of their relationship. It's an important metric as it costs less to keep an existing customers than it does to acquire new ones, so increasing the value of your existing customers is a great way to drive growth.

CHAPTER ELEVEN

The extraordinary life of challenging the status quo

*'Life is not a journey to the grave with the intention of
arriving safely in a pretty and well-preserved body. But
rather, to skid in broadside, thoroughly used up, totally
worn out, and loudly proclaiming'*

– author Mark Frost

I was discussing my first book, *Freedom After the Sharks*, with friends when one challenged me on what I'd written in Chapter Nine, "Building the Dream".

"So is it only successful people that take risks?" they asked me.

People who achieve greatness take calculated risks, and we all have the ability to make choices, but first we need to take a 'leap of faith'. Entrepreneurs do think things through and evaluate options. All ideas are researched to gain the foresight that is required to make an informed decision. But it generally comes down to the following three questions: What is the best-case scenario? What is the worst-case scenario? What is the most likely scenario?

As motivational speaker Denis Waitley once said: "Life is inherently risky. There is only one big risk you should avoid at all costs, and that is the risk of doing nothing." Taking risks is not the secret to life, but taking risks does mean we are never at risk of doing nothing. Too many people 'play it safe'. This is the playground of mediocrity. It is where average people live. They colour inside the lines, and always play by the rules. They fear the unknown, and rarely if ever venture outside the boundaries. People who 'play it safe' are predictable. Their life is run by rules and routine. Their actions are often dictated by the opinions of others. This is the crowd that fights to keep things the same.

Entrepreneurs are risk-takers; a different and extraordinary breed. They live in the realm of possibility and greatness. They are not afraid to live beyond the boundaries and to colour outside the lines. To them, there is no such thing as failure; only experiments that did not work. Risk-takers are marked by a sense of adventure and passion. They care little for the accolades of the crowd. They are more focused on squeezing everything they can out of every moment of time. They are not afraid to 'boldly go where no one has gone before'.

Think you can have success without risk? Think about it. Try naming one historical figure that made a difference by playing it safe and being average. The vast majority of successful people are remembered for the difference they made in their lifetime. And that difference required them to take risks and challenge the status quo.

We are inspired by people who go beyond the norm and push the boundaries of possibility. Mediocrity, on the other hand, does not inspire. Nor does it lead to greatness. Success, however you define it, will elude you unless you are willing to push the limits you have placed on yourself, and that others have placed on you.

The Orville brothers would never have made their historical flight if they had listened to the naysayers. Henry Ford would never have invented the automobile if he had paid attention to his critics. David would never have defeated Goliath if he had allowed his own family to discourage him. The list goes on and on.

Every major breakthrough in history, business, science, medicine, sports is the result of an individual who took a risk and refused to play it safe. Successful people understand this. Their innovation is the result of their adventurous spirit. They invent, achieve, surpass and succeed because they dare to live beyond the realm of normal.

Many people have mixed feelings about risk, in part because they sense that facing the things we fear can present solutions to our internal dilemmas. Risk is something you want and don't want, all at the same time. It tempts you with its rewards, yet repels you with its uncertainties.

Take off a diving board, for instance. It's been called a testament to man's indulgent pursuit of the insignificant. My own high-flying feats proved that I could withstand two and a half seconds of plummeting hell. So what? The answer lies in my confronting my limitations and fears. For me, taking a high dive was more than an act of bravado. It was an act of liberation.

Like it or not, taking risks is an inevitable and inescapable part of life. Whether you're grappling with the possibility of getting married, starting a business, making a high-stakes investment, or taking some other life or career leap of consequence, one of these days you'll wind up confronting your own personal high dive.

Risk makes us feel alive. Life without risk is life stuck in a rut. If you feel that your job or life is getting boring and monotonous, then you're not taking enough risk. We are built to take risk. We need change and growth in our lives. If you're not growing, then you're dying.

Nothing in this world truly stays the same.

Risk stretches us and helps us grow. Risk gets us out of our comfort zone to do something different. We learn by experience. Risk teaches us more about ourselves and helps us improve. How much more do we learn through the experiences of trying something big and failing? How much do you learn from taking risk and seeing the outcome?

Don't let your fear of failure stop you. Fear of failure is often the single biggest obstacle that prevents us from reaching our full potential. We worry about what will happen if/when we fail. Realise that failure is relative. While you may interpret something as a failure, someone else may see it as a valuable learning experience. Often, failure is only failure to the extent you see it that way. What if true failure meant wasting your talent? What if failure was delaying action and missing opportunities because you didn't take that risk?

Every organisation faces various risk elements while doing business. Business risk implies uncertainty in profits or danger of loss and the events that could pose a risk due to some unforeseen events in future, which causes business to fail.

Find your true calling. You feel most alive when you're doing what you were meant to do. We're not supposed to stay the same, but are charged with growing and developing. Everyone has greatness in them if they challenge themselves enough.

When you are faced with a decision and are wondering if it is worth the risk, it may help to ask yourself these questions:

- Am I risking more than I am able to sustain, physically, mentally, or emotionally, at this time?

- Will I be able to take this opportunity again at some other point?

- Are my fears based on real danger, or just on the fear of the unknown?

- What other possible opportunities do I risk by taking/not taking this opportunity?

- Is the risk of doing nothing greater than what I risk by taking this opportunity?

If we think about risks with these questions and process the risk of doing nothing, we are likely to make choices that seem risky, even crazy, to others, but make sense for each of us in our own lives.

The truth is that no matter how much we try to avoid risk and hide from pain, it will still find us, even if it is just in the form of regret. It's far better to weigh each risk for ourselves and decide which risks are right for us to take than to always let the fear of risks force us to take the risk of doing nothing.

CHAPTER TWELVE

The challenges of leadership and digital disruption

'By seizing the opportunities that disruption presents and leveraging hard times into greater success through out-working/out-innovating/out-thinking and out-working everyone around you, this just might be the richest time of your life so far'

– lawyer and writer Robin S Sharma

The pace of digital disruption has left 50 per cent of businesses and public sector organisations fearful or worried that their organisations will not be able to keep up with what is to come over the next five years.

As technology continues to transform business models, a new breed of corporate leader is emerging who is digitally savvy and assiduously curious. Rather than fearing change and obsessively trying to retain control, the most accomplished CEOs accept that for an organisation to compete globally and attract and retain the best talent, they must be highly collaborative, operationally focused and ruthlessly strategic.

It is not enough for businesses to simply be aware of digital advances; they must interpret what these could mean for them and how they might benefit. Senior executives of large organisations have many legitimate concerns and questions about the opportunity that digital presents.

Whether due to unclear monetisation models, baffling market valuations, inflexible IT systems or never-ending jargon and predictions, digital can certainly seem disruptive – and not always in a positive sense.

Despite a sea of uncertainty, it is becoming evident that organisations that successfully leverage digital technologies for new growth operate with a different set of rules and capabilities, and see greater returns.

This is a list of seven critical management concerns:

- Sensing and interpreting disruption

    Merely sensing change is not enough. The trick is to interpret what these changes mean to the business and, more importantly, when they will have an impact. If business leaders are unable to interpret these change signals, they are no better placed than those who did not see change coming. Research shows that half of business leaders expect competitors to change at least some part of their business model.

    The key question is: What will these new business models be, and when will they become relevant?

- Experimenting to develop and launch new ideas more quickly

    Ask most entrepreneurs about how they innovate and they may look nonplussed. Most digital disrupters do not see themselves as 'innovating', per se. In their minds, they are solving specific customer problems the best way they know how. As such, innovation is a consequence, not a goal.

Solving customer problems requires two actions: experimenting more and learning to self-disrupt. Digital technologies enable a new way of experimenting at almost an unlimited scale.

- Fully understanding and leveraging data

    Businesses hold almost unimaginable amounts of data, and are grappling with how to use it to develop new products and services that bring new value to their customers.

    Mastering the art of exploiting data, not only by turning it into useful information, but also by finding new ways to monetise it, will be fundamental to how businesses run in the future

- Building and maintaining a high digital quotient team

    While IQ and EQ measure intellectual and emotional intelligence respectively, thetime is ripe for DQ – a measure of the digital quotient (or digital savviness) of organisations. As companies evolve their digital capabilities, they need to measure and rapidly build their teams' DQ, not least among their senior members.

    Some organisations are pursuing a strategy of acquihiring or acqhiring: buying the right skills through acquisitions of technology start-ups, or by establishing formal relationships with the start-up community

- Partnering and investing in all non-core activities

  One of the characteristics of effective digital leaders is their intuitive understanding that the journey is not one to be undertaken alone. A recent report that I read indicated that companies will be increasing their partnerships and alliances as they attempt to boost digital growth in the next three years.

  Whether looking for new application programming interfaces (APIs), corporate development or business development partners, aligning with an ecosystem of partners is critical to digital progress. The more they invest in others, the more organisations extend the team that is as vested in their success as they are

- Organising for speed

  Two elements are essential for businesses to be organised for speed. The first is CEO-level support and the presence of a dedicated central team to drive new digital growth. The second is a team of 'fixers' – those at the centre of operations who are independent, respected and can draw on the right skills at the right time.

  Many organisations are establishing the role of chief digital officer (CDO) – a sound choice when that person also has the power to drive change and has responsibilities that are distinct from the chief information officer (CIO), chief risk officer (CRO) and chief marketing officer (CMO).

  New structures are emerging to help organisations respond more quickly to digital change. Banks have partnered with accelerators that help bring new ideas, while many retailers have set up venture funds to access disrupters.

Other companies have acquired digital teams to enhance their internal capabilities, often funding entrepreneurs who know little about their industry to create a start-up that could seriously hurt their respective businesses.

This counterintuitive process can reveal some implicit industry assumptions that are holding back the business

- Designing a delightful customer experience

  Customers' primary motivation for repeat business is the quality of their experience. Digital technologies have reset expectations here. Today, a banking customer using a mobile banking app does not compare it with apps from other banks, but against their best mobile user experiences for usability or functionality, whatever the industry.

  It's important that organisations put the customer at the heart of their business and stand in their shoes when designing beautiful customer experiences.

Digital technology has already broken down the old, familiar business models, but the effect it will have on the future of organisations' operations as it evolves remains significant and unknown. So, CEOs and business leaders are rightly concerned about keeping upwith speed and objectives.

You must embrace the change, or get left behind. While executives do not necessarily need to be literate in coding, it is imperative that they understand the role that digital technology plays in a modern organisation, especially if they are to realise the benefits of optimised productivity, efficiency and responsiveness to customers. In fact, according to McKinsey, a leading global management consulting company, 'Unlocking success in digital transformations' nine out of ten senior decision makers say digital technology is essential to a business's future success.

Meet your customer expectations before someone else does. Delivering good customer service has become more challenging due to an overwhelming consensus that digital, and a hyper-connected society, has changed customers' expectations. Business must adapt the way they do things to keep up.

Business-to-business organisations that may not have originally seen these consumer-focused demands as relevant to them are also feeling the pull, increasingly citing digital media as being very important from the perspective of recruiting talent, engaging colleagues and disseminating and sharing information across teams. As a modern day leader it is critical to understand not only what technology exists, but how to utilise it to satisfy consumers' and employees' ever-increasing expectations to drive a competitive advantage.

Remember: a modern workforce is a collaborative workforce. With the increase in the use of digital tools for working, boundaries are blurring and businesses are becoming more agile. To enable collaborative working, CEOs are turning to their CIOs, CROs and CDOs to make use of technology to achieve this.

By taking a more collaborative approach with all leaders in the business, digital can be used to transform business processes. By reaching out to the wider team, the CEO can unearth processes and areas of the business that could become more efficient and effective through digital technology, such as customer service and workflow management.

Consider digital as an enabler, not a disrupter. Having acknowledged that digital technology will play a central role in future success, business leaders cannot afford to show fear of it, or reluctance to implement it. Instead they must lead by example, embracing technology with a clear view of the potential advantages to be unlocked. Using technology to meet the rising expectations from the consumer is a must in today's marketplace. Business leaders need to first understand what customers expect and then make best use of the available technology to meet their customers' needs.

By embracing technology and using it in an innovative way, business leaders will be better positioned to maintain a competitive advantage by driving innovation, productivity and efficiency throughout the business.

Finally, when leaders move toward improving their observable behaviours, they have the extraordinary ability to positively influence employees to willingly become engaged. That's a powerful investment that pays dividends not only in developing good people, but by directly affecting the organisation's bottom line.

Leadership in today's world is a balanced mix of universal characteristics and digital leadership traits which has the potential to guide us through years of transformation with optimism and idealism. Technology continues to prove that it can be used for the benefit of mankind, but only if we set sail on the right course and with smart individuals that makeour journey, progress, and performance so much worthwhile.

CHAPTER THIRTEEN

Parallels between corporate environments and hummingbirds

> *'It is not the strongest of the species that survives, nor the most intelligent that survives. It is the one that is most adaptable to change'*
>
> – naturalist Charles Darwin

On a visit to my international business partner, Mark Herbert, in Oregon, I could not help but notice a group of very excited hummingbirds. Mark and I started to think about whether there are any parallels between the corporate world and the lives of hummingbirds.

Hummingbirds are one of the smallest birds in the species. They can fit into your tall cup of coffee and weigh less than a tennis ball (the smallest, the bee hummingbird, is 5cm long and weighs 2g). They are one of the most adaptive creatures around. Having one of the highest metabolisms in any animal, they can also go in a hibernation-like state to conserve energy when needed.

They are one of the most versatile animals on earth. The only bird that can fly both forward, backward, upside down and has the ability to hover in one place as needed. They are also one of the fastest animals on the planet, with recorded speeds of up to 54km per hour. That is faster than some of the best race horses around. And, if you did not know, hummingbirds actually inspired the creation of the helicopter.

There are a lot of things humans – and business leaders – can learn from the hummingbird, both from the story and around the real facts about it: perseverance, courage, innovation, adaptability, versatility, and defying all odds.

Each year a hummingbird will fly from North America to South or Central America, proceeding at an average rate of about 20 miles per day. They leave in in January or February and the southward migration is complete by late May. Banding studies show that each bird tends to return every year to the same place it hatched, even visiting the same feeders. The Rufous has the longest migration route of all hummingbirds – up to 3,000 miles (4.828km) – travelling from summer in Alaska to winter in Mexico.

Hummingbirds are associated with goddesses throughout the myths and legends of multiple cultures. In one Mayan legend, the hummingbird is the sun in disguise, trying to court a beautiful woman, who is the moon. Hopi and Zuni legends tell of hummingbirds helping humans by convincing the gods to bring rain. An Aztec legend tells of a god who, in the form of a hummingbird, flew to the underworld to be with a goddess, who later gave birth to the earth's first flower. A Native American hummingbird animal totem is said to aid in self-discovery and provide us the paths to self-expression and awareness.

They are both agile and adaptable. The Oxford dictionary defines 'agile' as nimble, supple, dexterous, acrobatic, graceful –

all qualities that organisations and leaders today certainly look at building, being and demonstrating.

It seems to me that there are leaders who are quite like hummingbirds in their approach to life and leadership. As a leader, your attitude will make you or break you. The right attitude can guide you through times of adversity with poise and grace and be a source of inspiration for others to emulate. And at the end of the day it is all about the dailydecisions you make.

Here are four considerations for a good attitude"

- What you choose to see

    As you look over the landscape of your business or organisation, do you see recession, fear and uncertainty, or do you see opportunity, growth, and new markets? What you choose to see speaks of your perceptions. Your perceptions are shaped by your attitude. That is not to say you are not mindful of the negatives that exist, but that you are making a choice not to be defined by them. If you are going to have an attitude of excellence, it begins with what you choose to see and ignoring the rest

- What you choose to believe

    The hummingbird chooses new life and growth over what is dead and gone. Your belief systems form the foundation of your personal growth and that of your leadership potential. What you choose to see formulates your perceptions, but your beliefs formulate how you live. This attitude is the deal breaker both personally and professionally and it truly matters.

What you choose to believe speaks of your passion. Your passions are a reflection of your attitude and that is a reflection of your heart. What you choose to believe may not always make sense at the time. Yet when you choose faith over fear, hope over despair, trust over doubt, forgiveness over resentment, and love over hate, you are living out an attitude of belief that will set you apart as a leader

- How you spend your time

The hummingbird spends its time seeking life and beauty. When your attitude is aligned with what you believe and what you see it makes how you spend your time an easier proposition. How you spend your time is all about priorities. Whether in business or in your personal life your priorities are a good indicator of a healthy attitude. Your time is your most valuable possession and a smart leader learns how to master it

- How you live your life

The vulture and the hummingbird, for better or worse, have made their choices and live their lives accordingly. Your attitude as a leader has consequences that will determine your altitude. The choice to have a good attitude is not always easy. Someone cuts you up in traffic, the deal you thought you were going to close doesn't happen, your earnings report falls short of expectations, a friend betrays you; these scenarios and more constantly challenge your resolve to have a good attitude.

How you live your life speaks of your purpose. Your attitude should be one of your strongest attributes that sustains you in the good times and what gives you the courage needed when times are tough. Make it your priority to live your life as a leader with purpose in your heart.

Leadership forces you to stay true to yourself and to recognise when you are at your best and when you are at your worst; the important thing is to stay focused and keep moving forward. We always learn that it is overcoming adversity that brings the most satisfaction, and that achievements are made more meaningful by the struggle it took to achieve them.

Like the hummingbird, anything is possible if you believe in yourself and if you set your mind and heart to it. If you want something badly enough, you must be prepared to go after it with everything you have, no matter the odds.

Change has a funny habit of teaching you much about yourself; it goes to the core of your own weaknesses, strengths and eccentricities. Leadership forces you to stay true to yourself and recognise times when you are at your best and worst; the key is to stay focused and to make decisions that will create continuous improvement. Even though this may be small, incremental change, it is positive change you can build upon even though you may be in quicksand.

The question is, how much do you truly want your dream?

CHAPTER FOURTEEN

Why forecasting is important

*'Practically, systemic thinking can be used to identify
problems, analyse their boundaries, design strategies and
policy interventions, forecast and measure their expected
impacts, implement them, and monitor and evaluate their
successes and failures'*
– Nestlé Americas VP Paul Polman

Many CEOs tell me they would seek more comfort and be more confident if they could keep better tabs on their financials. They have put their plans into place based on economic and market assumptions made a few months back, but will they break through the continual pain barriers to maintain and increase growth?

Any company seeking growth these days would be wise to include a sensitivity analysis as part of the balance sheet forecast. There are many ways to book financial actuals, and financial teams may want to spend some time determining the best processes for their companies.

In either good times or bad, approaching the future with a robust forecast is vital for all kinds of businesses. Other considerations should include politics, economics, global risks and customer behaviour:

- Politics

    The pollsters failed miserably to predict the outcome of the past two UK general elections, the Brexit referendum and the US presidential election.

    It's tempting to blame the influence of fake news posted on social networks, given that allegations of foreign interference via such media are rarely far from the headlines.

    But Ian Goldin, director of the programme of technological and economic change at the University of Oxford's Martin School, suggests that other forces are stronger. "The growing extremism we've seen is part of a broader set of factors, of which the web is an amplifier, not a cause," he says. "Change is accelerating and our social-security safety net is weakening. People are getting left behind more quickly and insecurity is growing. There is a distrust of authority and expertise. Because house prices, rents and transport costs have increased so much relative to their incomes, people are getting locked out of dynamic cities where unemployment is low, pay is relatively high and citizens are more comfortable with change and immigration."

    So where does that leave those whose job is to gauge public opinion and fore castelectoral outcomes accordingly?

- Economics

  The playwright George Bernard Shaw once said: "If all economists were laid end to end, they would still not reach a conclusion."

  More than 120 years after he co-founded the London School of Economics, his wry observation has lost little relevance.

  Paul Hollingsworth, senior UK economist at Capital Economics, agrees, noting that their profession has "taken a bit of a beating in recent years" for its failure to predict, among other things, the 2007/8 global financial crisis. "More emphasis needs to be placed on possible ranges of outcomes and the associated probabilities, to enable businesses to plan for the worst but hope for the best," he says.

  Andrew Goodwin, lead UK economist at Oxford Economics, believes that "a premium on adaptability" is the smart way forward. He explains: "We find that the best approach isto combine sophisticated tools with expert insight and to identify alternative scenarios."

  Tej Parikh, chief economist at the Institute of Directors, meanwhile, points to the value of "stronger intelligence-sharing and collaboration", especially among SMEs.

  Given that the Office for Budget Responsibility has dropped its 2018 GDP growth forecast from 1.6 per cent to 1.4 per cent, calculated circumspection – or what he calls "stress-testing organisations against an array of macroeconomic scenarios" – seems wise advice indeed

- Global risks

  "In many respects, it's becoming easier to assess business-related risk, owing to the increasing accessibility of open-source information and intelligence," says Phil Cable, co-founder and CEO of risk management firm Maritime Asset Security and Training. "Global competition has forced businesses to spread their wings and trade in places where they wouldn't otherwise go. But assessing personal risks and employees' safety, security and health concerns in places where western standards are limited is still challenging."

  The Ipsos Mori Global Business Resilience Trends Watch 2018 survey, conducted in partnership with medical and travel security services firm International SOS, revealed that 42 per cent of organisations had altered the travel arrangements of their employees in 2017 because of risk ratings pertaining to security threats and natural disasters.

  The silos we used to work in no longer apply. We can sell to places anywhere in the world, but there's a downside – a pandemic can now cause a financial crisis, for instance. Hurricane Sandy, had it been bigger, could have led to a global crash

- Customer behaviour

  Forecasting how the public might spend its hard-earned cash is a far better informed exercise than it ever has been. So says Steve King, co-founder and CEO of Black Swan, afirm that predicts consumer trends using what he calls "the world's most advanced database of consumer thought and opinion" – aka the internet.

"Never before have we lived in an age when so many people have shared so much information about themselves, or when this knowledge has been so readily accessible," King says. "It's going to be incredibly interesting to see how the development of disruptive connected technologies such as the internet of things will change our behaviour in unexpected ways."

To fully exploit the sheer volume of customer-related information to be found online,real-time monitoring and instant responses are imperative, he adds. "Micro-trends are effectively created and destroyed almost overnight now. Brands must start moving with the times and away from qualitative future-gazing. They need to adopt new platforms that continually analyse social trends and offer quantifiable, robust predictions powered by artificial intelligence and machine learning."

Many companies do not understand the strategic importance of forecasting. Having the right resources available at the right time is essential for efficient functioning. In today's tough business environment where businesses are trying to save costs it is necessary that every penny is saved. Forecasting is one way to save costs, as companies can guess future demand and can manage their resources accordingly. Any mismanagement in forecasting can lead to great losses in both small and large businesses. All large companies use forecasting when formulating their strategy because without it no decisions can be made.

It is true that no one can predict the future accurately, but forecasting can give a general idea about future on which present decisions can be made. It is therefore an important strategic tool for all businesses.

CHAPTER FIFTEEN

Why corporate governance should not be stored on your C drive

'The biggest determinant in our lives is culture: where we are born, what the environment looks like. But the second biggest determinant is probably governance; good governance or a certain kind of governance makes a huge difference in our lives'

– investor and philanthropist Nicolas Berggruen

Being a director is often challenging and potentially lucrative, but if the prospect of being sued is looming, it can be a lonely and alarming position.

Directors and officers cover (D&O) provides a suit of armour in the face of legal action, with an insurer stepping in to provide guidance at the first sign of a problem, and ensuring legal costs and damages are met.

According to Eleni Petros, commercial crime practice leader for broker Marsh: "Cyber risks are a key topic in many boardrooms and are driven onto the agenda by high profile data breaches, distributed denial of services attacks and rising ransomware and cyber extortion attacks.

In the digital age, threats are coming thick and fast and directors are now more frequently having to contend with cyber attacks and data breaches – these are not just issues that affect large organisations.

Directors and high-ranking officers in public and privately held corporations are under scrutiny like never before as they conduct business in an increasingly regulated and complex global business environment.

As regulatory authorities have responded to public and shareholder pressure in the wake of the credit crisis with more rules, heightened vigilance and tougher enforcement powers, corporate leaders find themselves exposed to even greater risks on a daily basis as they go about their roles.

The pressures on their time are vast, not least for non-executives, who frequently spend as little as 30 days a year working in the business, and for the many directors who sit on the boards of four or five companies.

Board directors generally receive information packs that they receive from the companies they run are either far too large, and make it difficult for board members to target the business-critical information, or that they tell directors far too little about the key issues.

Nevertheless, directors face sanctions that make them sit up and take notice, not least the threat of jail. Though probably the least likely outcome for corporate leaders, jail terms can be handed down for antitrust failings, insider trading, bribery and corruption, money laundering or sanctions violations.

There is also the very real concern of regulatory fines and penalties. And these penalties can extend to being prohibited from sitting on boards in the future: the SIF regime now means that directors of banks that perform badly, though not necessarily personally liable, can find themselves excluded from directorships in regulated businesses going forward.

Then, of course, there is the growing threat of civil actions, and particularly shareholder class actions, on both sides of the Atlantic. For antitrust violations in the US, the maximum jail term for executives is 10 years, and there are instances where officers and directors have served four-year terms.

These penalties apply equally to foreign nationals running companies with US operations as they do to those businesses headquartered in the States, and antitrust authorities around the world are increasingly adopting similar approaches.

There are now more than 120 regimes that pursue this conduct globally, with around a dozen of those imposing criminal sanctions for breaches.

The number of antitrust cases being dealt with by the enforcement agencies has increased exponentially in recent years, not least because the incentives for reporting incidences of wrongdoing have increased, encouraging whistle blowers and pushing companies to approach the authorities when they are alerted to issues within their own organisations.

This first-mover advantage can work to the detriment of directors, who may be implicated by the companies they work for when detailed investigations take place. It is increasingly important for directors and officers to work hard to set the compliance tone for the organisation from the top, by making it clear to employees what is expected of them, by setting an example, and by ensuring that the messages are communicated across, and become part of, the company.

The guidance published with the Bribery Act 2010 is just one example of express reference to the importance of 'tone at the top'.

Business leaders need to design and implement systems and controls that are appropriate to their organisation, and regularly review and test those systems to ensure they are delivering results. At the same time, compliance requires a bottom-up approach, such that the system ensures that regular requests for information are made of all levels of the business, and frequent enquiries are initiated and followed up.

Directors need to ensure that the information that they receive is both timely and appropriately prioritised, so that they know they have done their best to be on top of what is going on.

In today's environment, directors and officers also need to look out for themselves, which means that if they have questions they must not only raise them, but also pursue answers, and record the fact that they have done so.

Directors need to be assertive with their colleagues across the business. If they find themselves dealing with topics with which they are not comfortable, they should seek external advice. There were countless examples of directors of financial institutions telling Congressional hearings in the US that they didn't understand the collateralised debt obligation products that their banks were trading, but ignorance is not an excuse that will find favour with regulators.

The key message is that devoting time, resources and effort to the compliance programme is the best guarantee of success, and that the companies that have successfully introduced effective cultures have done so only as a result of sustained commitment.

Directors must take responsibility for introducing and maintaining a culture of compliance across their organisation, which means building the right structures; delivering regular training to employees, and particularly those in high-risk areas; setting up proper audit procedures that allow for deep-dive checks on a regular basis; and acting on discoveries in a timely and effective way.

Finally, an ever-growing list of mandatory and non-mandatory rules is ramping up the risks faced by directors and officers. The general trend is toward raising the level of care expected of D&Os and expanding their existing duties.

These higher standards increase the personal risks and liabilities for D&Os as they look to steer their organisations through the complexity of today's business challenges. As a consequence, at-risk senior executives are searching for more sophisticated D&O coverage.

In many instances it is not the personal liabilities of directors that have changed, nor what constitute illegal acts, but rather the appetite of enforcement agencies to hold directors and officers accountable. Reprimanding senior executives is increasingly seen as the most effective means of changing behaviour and preventing criminal and civil offences going forward.

The trend of rigorous enforcement particularly holds true when it comes to international criminal acts, including crimes committed against antitrust legislation, against the UK Bribery Act or America's Foreign and Corrupt Practices Act, or breaching international sanctions laws.

Whether you are a large corporation or a small business, reaffirming the significance of the role of good corporate governance should be a business imperative.

Corporate governance performed properly results in the protection of shareholder assets. Fortunately, many boards take on this difficult and challenging role and perform it well. They do so by, among other things, being active, informed, independent, involved, and focused on the interests of shareholders.

Good boards also recognise the need to adapt to new circumstances – such as the increasing risks of cyber attacks. To that end, board oversight of risk management is critical to ensuring that companies are taking adequate steps to prevent, and prepare for, the harms that can result from mis-appropriation of management.

Eleni Petros, commercial crime practice leader for broker Marsh states: There is no substitution for proper preparation, deliberation, and engagement with company related issues. Given the heightened awareness of these rapidly evolving risks, directors should take seriously their obligation to make sure that companies are appropriately addressing those risks.

CHAPTER SIXTEEN

Not enough time… too much work

'One of the greatest resources people cannot mobilise
themselves is that they try to accomplish great things. Most
worthwhile achievements are the result of many little things
done in a single direction'
– businessman and motivational speaker
Nido Qubein

I really enjoy meeting up with my colleagues and friends, especially when we engage in 'meaningful conversations', but just recently, and more than ever, the words, "I do not have enough time, I am on work overload and feel exhausted," seem to be a running theme with life in general. So the question is do we have enough focus, or are we taking on too many initiatives?

One of the most persistent challenges that people face these days is 'initiative overload' – driving themselves too hard and having too many projects and not enough time to get them done. If you've ever found yourself working long days and weekends, and still not feeling caught up with your workload, then you know what I mean.

We all know that a big reason for this overload is the surge in expectations that is tied to a technology-enabled and connected global economy. As email, texting, instant messaging, teleconferencing, and other electronic communications have become indispensable, people have grown conditioned to expect fast, if not instantaneous, responses to almost everything.

For example, a recent study from The Social Habit found that when consumers contact companies through social media, 42 per cent expect a response in one hour or less, and 67 per cent expect a response the same day. The same seems to be true with work assignments in companies. As customers, managers and even in our personal lives we expect much more rapid turnaround times. And as people try to act faster, their actions and the changes to the actions end up taking more and more time – and so less gets finished..

Sometimes boards of directors and leaders are unaware of all the initiatives under way and their impact on the organisation. In other cases, organisational politics conspires to let initiatives continue long after they should have run their course. Either way, overload can result in costly productivity and quality problems and employee burnout. With record low unemployment, companies that do not adjust the workload are also at risk of losing valuable talent.

So why does 'initiative overload' happen?

In my experience, companies often lack the means (and the will) to stop existing initiatives. Sometimes that is because they have no process for determining when to close things down. A project might have been vital for the business when it launched, but later the rationale no longer exists – and yet the funding and the work continue.

Leadership teams often engage in prioritisation exercises that define and communicate where people should focus their energy. However, they undermine those efforts if they don't also do the hard work of explicitly deciding what trade-offs to make and what has to stop.

For companies already experiencing 'initiative overload', focusing on the benefits of cutting back can make the path forward somewhat easier.

Organisations are at a great advantage when they learn how to say no, as Steve Jobs once put it, to the "hundred other good ideas that there are".

They can then use their creative and productive energy more wisely, foster greater employee commitment and loyalty, and accomplish more in the areas that really matter.

The fact is that we are subjected to thousands of distractions throughout the day. A study published in the Journal of Experimental Psychology found that you can be distracted simply by hearing or feeling your phone vibrate, even if you don't pick it up. Try putting your phone out of sight (and touch) for 10 minutes of uninterrupted productivity.

Modern technology has evolved to exploit our urgency addiction: email, Facebook, Twitter, WhatsApp, Instagram, and more will fight to distract you constantly. Turn off all your notifications. Choose to check these things when you have time, or allocate time to be distracted – say, during a break from work – and work through them together, saving time. It's not , but once you build the good habit of turning off notifications, you can actually get to work and be more productive.

Schedule your priorities and stick to them. Treat your highest priorities like flights you have to catch: give them a set time in advance and say no to anything that would stop you making that flight. It pays to unplug.

If you can be reached via smartphone, email, Twitter, Facebook or LinkedIn, you're too available and all these outlets are possible connections that can distract you from your purpose. Disconnect and watch as your productivity improve.

Your smartphone might be the biggest productivity-killer of all time. Most people just can't put the phone away. If your phone is connected online, the temptation to stay updated about almost everything is very high. If you can, put down that phone (or power it off) for a while when in the office and witness the effect that that can have on your level of productivity.

The basic principle of success is to focus. It is what makes the difference between those who are successful and those who are not, regardless of how much talent, resource, and energy that they have. The most accomplished and well-known people in history were known for something unique to them. Einstein pursued the theory of relativity – one of the most famous scientific theories of the 20th century – as if his whole life depended on it. Mozart was incredibly passionate about music. He was the very best for many generations before and after him. Even today, is there a second musician who could match his genius?

Spend most of your time on the right things, and the rest takes care of itself. It's not enough to just 'work hard'. Hard work is not necessarily a bad thing. But hard work can be a waste of your life when it's directed at the wrong cause. Decide what is good for you in the long term, and pursue it with all you've got. Each time you have something extra to do or an additional goal to pursue, you further split your power.

Remember: less is more. The key to focusing on the essentials in life and at work is to limit yourself to an arbitrary but small number of things, forcing yourself to focus on the important stuff and eliminate all else. When you are doing too much at a time, you are constantly switching from one task to another, being constantly interrupted, constantly distracted. Do less, clear away distractions, single-task, and get more done.

When you do too much, your work is spread thinner, you have lower quality, and people won't spread your work like they should. By doing less, you can create something remarkable. Something incredible worth sharing.

Prioritising and optimising your time during the day will give you more time to focus on what matters, accomplishing more in less time.

CHAPTER SEVENTEEN

Does your executive board need an entrepreneurial approach to business?

*'This defines entrepreneur and entrepreneurship – the
entrepreneur always searches for change, responds to it, and
exploits it as an opportunity'*
– management consultant and author
Peter Drucker

There has been much discussion around transformative innovation that explores new horizons and potentially disrupts business models, and whether this requires an entrepreneur mindset on the board of directors.

This subject is increasing in board discussions and agendas, which has prompted me to take a closer look at the positives and repercussions of adapting an entrepreneurial approach to business.

If you are leading a start-up business or are involved in a scale-up business with potential for high growth, one of the most valuable things you should do early on is to set up an board of advisors. Scaling an enterprise is hard work, and you only stand to benefit from drawing on perspectives, experience, and networks that augment your own. A group of advisors committed to your success not only provides a sounding board to test and strengthen your ideas, it gives you access to important competencies and resources.

But many entrepreneurs, especially those in the early stages, find the task of building an advisory board daunting. Whose strengths will complement your own and counter your weaknesses? Who might bring an insight to the table that would otherwise be missed? It can feel like an exercise in knowing what you do not know. Moreover, most people who have not formalised such a board before have not given much thought to what it takes to keep one running effectively.

Board members tend to have immense experience in at least one of these three areas: financial expertise, industry-specific knowledge, or operational management. Over the past couple of decades, companies have become more interested in diversifying their boardroom, both in terms of race and gender as well as in expertise. Today, you'll find individuals with backgrounds in marketing, IT, and human resources in addition to the 'classic' board member tracks.

The latest trend, however, is adding someone with an entrepreneurial background to your team of directors. Boards are constantly being pulled between short term goal-oriented oversight and long term, strategically focused planning. Entrepreneurs are generally going to default to strategic thinking and will help pull your board out of conversations that should be left to your company's C-suite.

Entrepreneurs are often "visionaries" in the business world and offer a complementary element to boards that already favour members who are well-versed inrisk management or short term, operational guidance. This is not to say that an entrepreneur will always be right about their theories or suggestions, but their presence alone will force more conservative members to tackle some out-of-the-box thinking.

The boardroom is not generally thought of as the 'nerve centre' of entrepreneurism within a company, particularly a company trading on the stock exchange. The role of a typical director is often more about audit, risk reviews and compliance, and directors may see 'entrepreneurship' as a risk element. Often risk means keeping one or even both eyes on the rear-view mirror, and yet maybe the biggest threat is ahead and not yet fully visible in the headlights.

Most directors have little experience or understanding of the risks posed by disrupters and technological changes. With many directors on stock exchange companies being recruited from large and established companies, few of them can boast about any entrepreneurial experience. This raises a number of questions:

- Do boards need to be more entrepreneurial to detect and counter modern-day risks?

- Could a board that is more diverse in terms of experience, age or culture help address this?

We live in a fast paced and rapidly changing world. Even just a decade ago, changes to markets and business challenges were slower paced. However, since the dawn of global connectivity, big data and the maturing of the internet, companies are encountering threats at a much faster pace and competition is global.

Companies face modern-day risks associated with the Sharing Economy, cybercrime or even the IoT (Internet of Things). The threat posed by disrupters can be catastrophic and quickly bring down what was a very successful company. The board needs to anticipate changes and be innovative in relation to these modern day risks; that is, it has to become more entrepreneurial.

Yet, although the environment in which companies now operate is constantly changing, the behaviours of directors and the majority of boards are not. Boards spend significant time on compliance and on examining historical data on company performance and comparisons to budgets, yet the role of strategy sometimes remains an annual event completed, printed and filed away for 12 months.

Directors spend limited time considering strategy at a typical board meeting, and may regard innovation as a change of state and, therefore, a risk factor. Directors have a duty of care to their shareholders and are responsible for determining the company's growth and survival strategies. But do boards spend enough time discussing competition, or new developments in technology, or even possible changes to regulations that may in the future impact the business? For many boards, these areas are never discussed.

In the business world, will we ever forget Kodak and its devastating collapse, after being a highly successful business that neglected the need to change when digital photography came along? The irony is that the technology was originally developed by Kodak in 1975 and was effectively discarded because Kodak feared it threatened its photographic film business. Digitisation marched on, and, at the time, much smaller companies took it on, and everything else is now history. Although this is a classic example – and a tragic one for Kodak's shareholders and staff –

there are many other examples and are likely to be increasingly many more to come.

The new disruptive technologies of the sharing economy such those used by Uber and Airbnb are having a significant impact on the market value of companies in transport and hospitality. We should also consider the changes that have occurred in print media, including the retrenchment of many journalists because of the impact of digital media and resulting decline in advertising revenue. And then there's the decline of Blockbuster video and the rise of Netflix.

These types of disruptions in other industries could have staggering implications across many markets. In the area of banking and finance, for example, with the rise of high-growth, disruptive fintech companies, people are starting to collaborate to exchange money and bypass banks' foreign exchange departments.

Directors need to better understand threats and also assess more innovative growth strategies if their companies are to compete in the rapidly changing world in which we live. This means a different set of skills are needed at board level, in addition to the more traditional skills. Business survival requires boards and directors to be more agile and predictive, particularly in relation to disrupters that could be catastrophic for their business.

Technological advances and customer behaviour can turn the business fortunes of companies around very quickly. For the modern-day director, it is necessary to be constantly aware of the external environment so that potential disrupters can be quickly detected and countered.

As a result, more effort is needed to create an entrepreneurial approach at director level through properly managed processes and structures. This may include extending the current standard board committee structure to include a standalone innovation committee, providing leadership in innovation, and bringing in a structured process to manage and assess opportunities and threats.

Many classic-minded board members are extremely risk averse and for good reason. They are tasked with a great amount of responsibility to shareholders and to the overall success of an organisation. Unfortunately, this can sometimes lead them to fear failure in such a way that it stifles success. Many successful entrepreneurs are known for embracing small failures in order to reach large triumphs. This attitude in support of both flexibility and evolution brings a unique and forward-thinking element to any boardroom.

With the growing need for businesses to fend off disruptions, as well as to create their own disruptions, it is time to consider how board meetings can evolve so that instead of spending so much time on backwardlooking and historical data, boards do a little bit of creative forecasting and consider the future of the business and the market. Some suggestions are:

- Create an innovation committee

    Increasing the time spent considering innovation will make an enormous difference to many companies

- Spend some time discussing 'what if' scenarios to facilitate innovation discussions

    Develop an opportunity management focus at the board level, instead of just a riskmanagement focus

- Place on the board's agenda an item for competitive trends and behaviours and possible disruptions to the business model

    Look to other industries for examples of how disruptions have been addressed

- Encourage management to look to untapped knowledge in the staff pool

    Users of the 'sharing economy' might have a good understanding of disrupters. And, when it comes to funding a company, maybe consider other innovative methods to raise funds

The future is bright for those who direct their focus to the headlights and away from the rear-view mirror. Being forewarned of an impending risk or threat may provide the opportunity to develop strategies and so mitigate that threat before its impact is catastrophic. Keeping an eye on what is coming may help enable your company to be the disrupter, not the disrupted. Maybe we all need to reflect on that 'Kodak Moment' to see how quickly things can change.

To achieve substantial and continued growth in the 21st century, companies will have to look beyond improving the existing business model or simply launching new products. These actions just will not generate enough growth any more. Growth will come from more ambidextrous organisations that excel at improving their established business model (exploitation) and at inventing tomorrow's growth engines at the same time (exploration).

CHAPTER EIGHTEEN

Does (and should) shareholder value rule business?

'As we continue to drive the benefits of integrating our enterprise skills, capabilities, and experience – what we call operating as 'One Boeing' – we will find new and better ways to engage and inspire employees, deliver innovation that drives customer success, and produce results to fuel future growth and prosperity for all our stakeholders'

– Boeing CEO, president and chairman
Dennis Muilenburg

What is the purpose of a corporation? It's remarkable that after a century of management theorising, there is no agreed upon answer.

Common sense tells us that the purpose of a business is to make money. A conversation with almost any businessman or economist shows it to be so. Why else would a company be in business? Many experts agree: *The Economist* has recently declared that the goal of maximising shareholder value, ie making money for shareholders, is "the biggest idea in business". Today, it says, "shareholder value rules business".

Yet two distinguished Harvard Business School professors – Joseph L Bower and Lynn S Paine – recently declared in Harvard Business Review that maximising shareholder value is "the error at the heart of corporate leadership". It is "flawed in its assumptions, confused as a matter of law, and damaging in practice," they say. Bower has long held this view: back in 1970, he told National Public Radio that maximising shareholder value was "pernicious nonsense".

Jack Welch, who in his tenure as CEO of GE from 1981 to 2001 was seen as the uber-hero of maximising shareholder value, has been even harsher. In 2009, he declared that shareholder value is "the dumbest idea in the world. Shareholder value is a result, not a strategy... your main constituencies are your employees, your customers and your products. Managers and investors should not set share price increases as their overarching goal... Short-term profits should be allied with an increase in the long-term value of a company."

Despite these denunciations, the "pernicious nonsense" of shareholder value has spread. Shareholder-value thinking, say Bower and Paine, "is now pervasive in the financial community and much of the business world. It has led to a set of behaviours by many actors on a wide range of topics, from performance measurement and executive compensation to shareholder rights, the role of directors, and corporate responsibility." There are thus two opposing schools of thought: shareholder value is either the best idea in business or the worst idea in the world. Which is it?

Corporate strategy is the overall plan of contemporary management practice. CEOs have been obsessed with diversification since the early 1960s, because almost no consensus exists about what corporate strategy is, much less about how a company should formulate it.

A diversified company has two levels of strategy: business unit (or competitive) strategy and corporate (or company-wide) strategy. Competitive strategy is concerned with how to create competitive advantage in each of the businesses in which a company competes. Corporate strategy asks two different questions: what businesses the corporation should be in, and how the corporate office should manage the array of business units. Corporate strategy is what makes the corporate whole add up to more than the sum of its business unit parts.

The track record of corporate strategies has been dismal. A study of the diversification records of 33 large and prestigious US companies from 1950-1986 found that most had divested many more acquisitions than they had kept. In addition, the corporate strategies of most companies have dissipated rather than created shareholder value.

The need to rethink corporate strategy could hardly be more urgent. By taking over companies and breaking them up, corporate raiders thrive on failed corporate strategy. Fuelled by junk bond financing and growing acceptability, raiders can expose any company to takeover, no matter how large or blue chip.

Recognising past diversification mistakes, some companies have initiated large-scale restructuring programmes. Others have done nothing at all. Whatever the response, the strategic questions persist. Those who have restructured must decide what to do next to avoid repeating the past; those who have done nothing must awake to their vulnerability. To survive, companies must understand what good corporate strategy is.

Many post-Enron discussions about corporate governance have focused almost exclusively on the responsibilities of directors and the structure of boards and shareholders. This is hardly surprising – after all, a company's survival ultimately depends on the effectiveness of its board's decision-making processes. But boards don't exist in a vacuum. Ultimately, board structures and decision-making cultures will depend on a company's unique circumstances.

Large companies may also operate different levels of boards throughout their businesses. The complexity of large international organisations with many subsidiaries makes the issue of management information and decision-making more complex, and the need for directors of such vast organisations to have early-warning systems is a must.

The board of directors in any organisation is responsible for its operational, strategic and financial performance, as well as its conduct. Boards exercise their responsibilities by clearly setting out the policy guidelines within which they expect the management to operate. They will set out the short- and long-term objectives of the organisation and a system for ensuring that the management acts in accordance with these directions.

They will also put procedures in place for measuring progress towards corporate objectives. There is therefore a clear difference between the main responsibilities of directors and managers.

In his recent book, *Corporate Governance and Chairmanship: A Personal View*, Sir Adrian Cadbury distinguishes between direction and management: "It is the job of the board to set the ends – that is to say, to define what the company is in business for – and it is the job of the executive to decide the means by which those ends are best achieved." They must do so, however, within rules of conduct and limits of risk that have been set by the board.

Can your board answer the following strategic questions?:

- Who are our stakeholders?

- What are our stakeholders' stakes?

- What opportunities and challenges do stakeholders present?

- What economic, legal, ethical, and social responsibilities does our organisation have towards our various stakeholders?

- What strategies or actions should we take to best manage stakeholder challenges and opportunities?

- Do we have a system for managing relationships with stakeholders?

- How do we measure results? What metrics do we use to assess and gauge stakeholder relationships?

- In a crisis how quickly can we communicate with our relevant stakeholders?

- Do we know the various methods to engage with stakeholders and when not to use them?

- Can we state how much we are spending on each stakeholder group and what our ROI is?

- Have we developed a set of rules and practices on how best to manage the process of building stakeholder reputation with each stakeholder group?

Once you have answered the above questions, then you should attempt these:

- What strategies or actions should our firm take to best manage stakeholder challenges and opportunities?

- Should we deal directly or indirectly with stakeholders?

- Should we take the offence or the defence in dealing with stakeholders?

- Should we accommodate, negotiate, manipulate or resist stakeholder overtures?

- Should we employ a combination of the above strategies or pursue a singular course of action?

Shareholder value has been called the driving force of 21st century business. But what value do shareholders bring to the companies they invest in? Are most shareholders interested in what is best for the company, or are they in it only for the financial performance of the company's shares?

Regenerative capitalism is an alternative framework

for capitalism that embodies a deeper purpose than merely optimising financial returns, with the goal of promoting the long-term health and wellbeing of our human communities and the planet. Aligned with the latest understanding of how the universe works, the collaboratively created framework illuminates eight key principles backed by solid science and transdiciplinary scholarship.

Adam Smith, the founder of capitalism, said that everyone should do what is best for themselves. However, Professor Nash, portrayed in the movie A Beautiful Mind, starring Russell Crowe, stated that "Adam Smith was wrong!"

Commercial organisations can only succeed if everybody is doing what is best for themselves while simultaneously doing what best for the whole group. Beginning in the 1990s, we witnessed extreme egocentric behaviour among public companies who were motivated solely by their own financial gains. Several studies by Arcada prove that self-centred and egocentric companies perform poorly as compared to companies who focus on developing innovative products, delivering value for the customer, and motivating their employees to be more productive and successful.

How can these companies deliver value to their customers or suppliers if they are only looking at their own bottom line? Too much focus on shareholder value, measured by quarterly reports, is one of the primary reasons that public companies are not realising their full potential and that the West has been in financial chaos for the past six years.

Companies that outperform the rest – over time – build their success on a performance-based culture, driven from the outside in. Most executives agree that it's important to create value for the customer. The problem is that despite the good intentions of the senior management team, this mindset often doesn't travel farther than the company core values posted in the reception lobby of the corporate headquarters. You know the classic four: honesty, engagement, customer focus, and collaboration. If you exchanged one company's value statement for the values posted in the lobby of the corporate headquarters across the street, would anyone notice? Or are the values posted in the lobby of the neighbouring company the same four?

Professor Solow, winner of the Nobel Prize for his theory on economic growth, found that only a portion of financial growth in the world comes from companies making money out of money. Instead, the majority of financial growth comes from companies actually producing a product, developing a new service, or changing the way we conduct business.

Corporate leaders need to do more than shuffle numbers on a balance sheet. Consider Steve Jobs' unrelenting focus on product innovation and what Apple was able to achieve by creating the iPad, iPhone, and iPod. As we know, iTunes has literally changed the entire music industry.

The obsession with maximising shareholder value has also impacted the way that companies approach negotiations with their customers and suppliers. To solve the world's economic crisis, we need brave CEOs and leaders to step up and declare, "I don't care what the share value will be for the next two years. We might not make a profit during this period. But we are going to focus all our resources on product research and development with the goal to create the best product the world has ever seen. We're here to change the world! We are fully committed to delivering value and a return on investment to our shareholders. Yet it may not be in the next 30 days or even the next three quarters. I am asking our investors to look at us with a long-term view. I am asking them to stand by us and risk a much larger return on their investment if they will agree to fund the innovation required to develop a market-changing product."

If you left a stack of Sharpies piled beneath the statement of core values that hangs in the lobby of your company, what kind of graffiti would you find scribbled on your values statement? What would your customers and suppliers write? Your corporate values are better articulated by your employees, customers, and strategic partners than by your management team and board of directors. If there is a disconnect between your formal statement of values and the graffiti, you have work to do.

If you can build a product that will truly change the world, like Steve Jobs did several times, your shareholder value will take care of itself. Your problems will be protecting your distribution channels, defending your intellectual property, and retaining your talent. Which set of problems would you prefer? I think the answer is obvious – to hell with shareholder value.

Experience tells us that listening to your stakeholders and striving to meet their expectations, therefore ensuring that they feel heard, valued, and appreciated, grows trust, support and credibility. Building relationships and understanding motivation takes time and effort but will make your job easier in the long run. Companies are more successful when everyone is on board and on the same page.

CHAPTER NINETEEN

What is required to be an effective leader in today's totally disruptive business world?

> *'We can't solve our problems from the same level of thinking that created them'*
> – theoretical physicist Albert Einstein

A running theme that seems to be on every leadership and executive director's mind is 'What is required to be an effective leader in today's totally disruptive business world?' Experts at Harvard University have opined for decades on the reasons behind the spectacular failure rates of strategy execution. In 2016, it was estimated that 67 per cent of well-formulated strategies failed due to poor execution. There are many explanations for this abysmal failure rate, but a 10-year longitudinal study on executive leadership showed one clear reason. A full 61 per cent of executives said they were not prepared for the strategic challenges they faced on being appointed to senior leadership roles. It is no surprise, then, that 50-60 per cent of executives fail within the first 18 months of being promoted or hired.

Becoming a disruptive leader is not a straightforward journey, no matter your background. It requires the embrace of wholesale change, the nurturing of innovative thinking and behaviour, and the management of outcomes rather than resources. It requires a personal transformation that many will choose not to make. Over the past year, I've been struck by how many times I have heard C-suite leaders use these words (wholesale change, innovative thinking and behaviour, and managing outcomes) – or very similar ones – to describe the strengths they believe are critical to transforming their businesses, and to competing effectively in a disruptive era.

What's equally striking is how difficult organisations are finding it to embed these qualities and behaviours in their people. That's because the primary obstacle is invisible: the internal resistance that all human beings experience, often unconsciously, when they're asked to make a significant change. Cognitively, it shows up as mindset – fixed beliefs and assumptions about what will make us successful and what won't. Emotionally, it usually takes the form of fear.

A few years ago, digital disruption was something that happened to someone else. Amazon changed how we buy things. Netflix transformed how we consume videos. And companies like Airbnb and Uber shook up the hotel and transportation industries. Now, no company is immune. Disruptive technologies, products, services and business models are being introduced almost daily. So executives need to take charge of their organisation's response to ensure long-term business success.

But while many organisations are eager to 'get ahead of the curve' on digital, there's no instruction manual or template for how to do it successfully. A recent KPMG survey of chief executives and chief information officers found that while most are concerned about digital disruption, few are adequately prepared to address it.

Although digital may be disrupting your business model, it also creates opportunities for those that embrace change. Organisations that don't will find it increasingly difficult to catch up as technology continues to advance rapidly. So where do you start?

First, understand how digital disruption is affecting your products, services and business model. Then develop a digital strategy. That includes acquiring the necessary digital skills and getting the company to buy into the required changes.

KPMG's CIO Advisory survey shows this won't be easy. The majority of CIOs (58 per cent) and almost half of the CEOs (43 per cent) said they are involved or very involved in their firm's digital business strategy. But only a small number are actively leading the effort.

Given the magnitude of digital disruption, the lack of strong leadership could have a major impact on a company's ability to adapt. Companies must master and implement new technologies. That requires new skills, many of which are in short supply. Most CIOs in the KPMG survey cited a lack of critical skills and the limits of existing IT systems as their biggest challenges.

There are no quick solutions to these challenges. But first companies need to develop a strategy. Without one, it is impossible to tackle the other issues. The complexity of the challenges that organisations face is running far out ahead of the complexity of the thinking required to address them.

Consider the story of the consultant brought in by the CEO to help solve a specific problem: the company is too centralised in its decision-making. The consultant has a solution: decentralise. Empower more people to make decisions. And so it is done, with great effort and at great expense. Two years pass, the company is still struggling, and a new CEO brings in a new consultant. We have a problem, the CEO explains. We're too decentralised. You can guess the solution.

Rare is the business executive who doubts the importance of responsiveness: when (re-)designing the organisation structure, they tend to decentralise decision-making, so that decision rights are as close as possible to the people who deal with customers, competitors, front-line employees, and other stakeholders. The primary challenge most large companies now face is disruption, the response to which requires a new strategy, new processes, and a new set of behaviours. But if employees have long been valued and rewarded for behaviours such as practicality, consistency, self-reliance and prudence, why wouldn't they find it uncomfortable to suddenly embrace behaviours such as innovation, agility, collaboration and boldness?

Human development is about progressively seeing more. Learning to embrace our own complexity is what makes it possible to manage more complexity.

CHAPTER TWENTY

Have we forgotten leadership and the foundation of business planning?

'When we tackle obstacles, we find hidden reserves of courage and resilience we did not know we had. And it is only when we are faced with failure do we realise that these resources were always there within us. We only need to find them and move on with our lives'

– aerospace scientist and president of India

APJ Abdul Kalam

One of the questions I hear frequently from emerging and current leaders is: "How has leadership changed from 10 years ago, and what do I need to understand about running a successful enterprise that I don't know today?"

Leadership has definitely changed. So much so, in fact, that today, according to McKinsey in its report Organisation at Scale, only 14 per cent of CEOs have the leadership talent to execute their strategy.

Data from the EY Global Leadership Forecast 2018 shows that organisations with effective leadership talent outperform their peers. Yet very few organisations manage this high-value asset in an integrated, cohesive way. Even after spending more than $50billion annually on developing their leaders, many companies still don't have the bench strength to meet their future business goals. And despite the spending, investments are often fragmented and see a lack of returns.

Leadership models and development programmes abound; yet few tie in to business goals. Worse yet, there's scant evidence that they actually work. What's needed is a coherent, integrated leadership strategy.

A well-crafted blueprint ensures that companies have the right talent, at the right cost, and with the right capabilities to deliver today and into the future. Yet, the EY Global Leadership Forecast 2018 report found less than one-third of the HR professionals surveyed feel their organisations have an effective leadership strategy. Companies that do have such strategies in place report better returns on their investment in talent. They consistently feature deeper leader bench strength and stronger leaders at all levels.

Many leaders are living with an identity crisis. They are uncertain about how to lead in a more diverse, transient, multigenerational environment that requires them to embrace diversity of thought – and they fail to see the potential opportunities this represents to both workplace and marketplace success.

When leaders become too comfortable with a one-size-fits-all approach to leadership, they conversely become uncomfortable with the uncertainty and change that more successful leaders embrace as part of the job. Complacent leaders are at risk of becoming irrelevant because they are unable or unwilling to course correct their style, approach and attitude to the environment of change they must lead through.

Leaders fail in their primary role and responsibility of enabling the full potential in people and the business they serve because they don't know the difference between substitution and evolution. Instead of leading the organisation and its people to continually evolve, they get stuck in a cycle of complacency and the substitution of activities associated with it. As a result, the company cannot grow or its growth cannot be sustained.

The result is a major shortfall in competent, cluedup global leaders. According to a 2017 report by Price Waterhouse Coopers, 75 per cent of hiring managers believe leadership skills are hard to find in new recruits. And a Deloitte study found a whopping 87 per cent of companies aren't effective at building global leaders.

What could be more vital to a company's long-term health than the choice and cultivation of its future leaders? And yet, while companies maintain meticulous lists of candidates who could at a moment's notice step into the shoes of a key executive, an alarming number of newly minted leaders fail spectacularly, ill prepared to do the jobs for which they supposedly have been groomed.

Look at Coca-Cola's Douglas Ivester, longtime CFO and Robert Goizueta's second in command, who became CEO after Goizueta's death. Ivester was forced to resign in two and a half years, thanks to a serious slide in the company's share price, some bad public-relations moves, and the poor handling of a product contamination scare in Europe.

You have all possibly read the Harvard Business Review "Bench Strength: Grooming Your Next CEO", on Mattel's Jill Barad, whose winning track record in marketing catapulted her into the top job – but didn't give her insight into the financial and strategic aspects of running a large corporation.

Ivester and Barad failed, in part, because although each was accomplished in at least one area of management, neither had mastered more general competencies such as public relations, designing and managing acquisitions, building consensus, and supporting multiple constituencies. They're not alone. The problem is not just that the shoes of the departed are too big; it's that succession planning, as traditionally conceived and executed, is too narrow and hidebound to uncover and correct skill gaps that can derail even the most promising young executives.

Harvard Business School released some research into the factors that contribute to a leader's success or failure. It found that certain companies do succeed in developing deep and enduring bench strength by approaching succession planning as more than the mechanical process of updating a list. Those companies have combined two practices, succession planning and leadership development, to create a long-term process for managing the talent roster across their organisations. In most companies, the two practices reside in separate functional silos, but they are natural allies because they share a vital and fundamental goal: getting the right skills in the right place.

To succeed in the 21st century workplace and marketplace, leaders must come out from under their identity crisis and embrace diversity of thought so that those they lead can overcome their own identity crises and reach their full potential. They must embrace risk and change as opportunities that others may fail to see as such. And they especially must understand the difference between substitution and evolution: one leads to the trap of complacency, the other leads to a path of growth and continued success. In the end, the wise leader knows their subject matter and is confident in understanding how their leadership identity supports of the organisation's evolution.

Perhaps the underlying lesson is that good succession management is possible only in an organisational culture that encourages candour and risk-taking at executive level. It depends on a willingness to differentiate individual performance and a corporate culture in which the truth is valued more than politeness.

CHAPTER TWENTY-ONE

Why leadership matters

> '*Coming together is a beginning; keeping together is
> progress; working together is success. Failure is simply the
> opportunity to begin again, this time more intelligently.
> Whether you think you can, or you think you can't –
> you're right. Anyone who stops learning is old, whether at
> 20 or 80*'
>
> – industrialist Henry Ford

As all leaders experience the highest of highs and the lowest of lows, you will know you have been tested in ways that you never expected. And yet, somehow, you prevail.

Despite the frustrations, anger and fear, you will have learned a lot about yourself. You will be be forced to recognise your own weaknesses and eccentricities, and discover reserves of strength that you had not known existed. In the process, you will become less judgmental and more accepting of yourself and of others.

Leadership forces you to stay true to yourself and to recognise when you are at your best and when you are at your worst; the important thing is to stay focused and keep moving forward.

You will learn that overcoming adversity is what brings the most satisfaction, and that achievements are made more meaningful by the struggle it took to achieve them.

Leadership will conquer; this is the most profound truth of your individual journey. With courage, drive, determination, resilience, imagination, energy and the right team, you will find success. Winston Churchill once said: "This is not the end. It is not even the beginning of the end. But it is, perhaps, the end of the beginning."A single brain sometimes cannot take decisions alone. One needs the assistance and guidance of others as well to accomplish the tasks within the desired time frame. In a team, every member contributes to their level best to achieve the assigned targets. The team members must be compatible with each other to avoid unnecessary conflicts and misunderstandings.

Every team should have a team leader who can hold their team together and extract the best out of the members. The team leader should inspire every individual and give advice and guidance whenever required. A leader should be a role model for their team members and a great mentor.

I had the pleasure of meeting Brendan Hall – he led the *Spirit of Australia* yacht crew to overall victory in the 2009/10 Clipper Round the World Race, when he was 28. It was the second of three times the trophy has gone to an Australian team.

Following the win, Brendan wrote the book *Team Spirit*, based on his race insights into the teamwork, leadership, skill, courage and focus required for performance.

Brendan told me how his team had just faced the ultimate challenge and one that they could never have been prepared for.

Circumstances dictated that he had to get off their boat to help another vessel, and the *Spirit of Australia* crew had to sail across the world's largest ocean at a particularly fearsome time of year, on their own, with no skipper on board.

"They pulled together in the true sense of teamwork, and kept each other safe," Brendan says. "I feel it was their greatest achievement, and it was mine by association as I had got them to the point where they could take on that challenge. Ultimately that experience and those qualities led to our overall result." During the race, his crew had the same raw materials as every other boat. They had characters and influential people and leaders; together they made a great leadership team.

The approach Brendan took was to empower everybody throughout the race and the goal was to get to a point where Brendan was redundant on deck and he could concentrate on everything else, such as weather routeing and the navigation.

A true team leader plays an important role in guiding team members and motivating them to stay focused. Every team is formed for a purpose. The leader alone should not set the goal; suggestions should be invited from one and all and issues must be discussed in an open forum. They must make their team members well aware of their roles and responsibilities. They must understand their team members well. The duties and responsibilities must be assigned as per their interest and specialisation for them to accept the challenge willingly.

Never impose things on your team. Encourage the team members to help each other. Create a positive ambience at the workplace. Avoid playing politics or provoking individuals to fight. Make sure that the team members do not fight among themselves. In case of conflict, don't add fuel to the fire; rather try to resolve things immediately. Listen to both parties before coming to any conclusion. Try to come up with an alternative that is feasible for all.

The following five reasons summarise the importance of teamwork and why it matters:

- Teamwork motivates unity in the workplace

    A teamwork environment promotes an atmosphere that fosters friendship and loyalty.

    These close-knit relationships motivate employees in parallel and align them to work harder, co-operate and be supportive of one another.

    Individuals possess diverse talents, weaknesses, communication skills, strengths, and habits. Therefore, when a teamwork environment is not encouraged this can pose many challenges towards achieving the overall goals and objectives. This creates an environment where employees become focused on promoting their own achievements and competing against their fellow colleagues. Ultimately, this can lead to an unhealthy and inefficient working environment.

    When teamwork is working the whole team is motivated and working towards thesame goal in harmony

- Teamwork offers perspectives and feedback

    Good teamwork structures provide your organisation with a diversity of thought, creativity, perspectives, opportunities, and problem-solving approaches. A proper team environment allows individuals to brainstorm collectively, which in turn increases their success to problem solve and arrive at solutions more efficiently and effectively.

Effective teams allow the initiative to innovate, in turn creating a competitive edge to accomplish goals and objectives. Sharing differing opinions and experiences strengthens accountability and can help make effective decisions faster than when done alone.

Team effort increases output by having quick feedback and multiple sets of skills come into play to support your work. You can do the stages of designing, planning, and implementation much more efficiently when a team is functioning well

- Teamwork provides improved efficiency and productivity

When incorporating teamwork strategies, you become more efficient and productive.

This is because they allows the workload to be shared, reducing the pressure on individuals, and ensure tasks are completed within a set time frame. Teamwork also allows goals to be more attainable, enhances the optimisation of performance, improves job satisfaction and increases work pace.

Ultimately, when a group of individuals work together, compared to one person working alone they promote a more efficient work output and are able to complete tasks faster due to many minds being focused on the same goals and objectives of the business

- Teamwork provides great learning opportunities

    Working in a team enables us to learn from one another's mistakes. You are able to avoid future errors, gain insight from differing perspectives, and learn new concepts from more experienced colleagues. In addition, individuals can expand their skill sets, discover fresh ideas from newer colleagues and therefore ascertain more effective approaches and solutions towards the tasks at hand. This active engagement generates the future articulation, encouragement and innovative capacity to problem solve and generate ideas more effectively and efficiently

- Teamwork promotes workplace synergy

    Mutual support, shared goals, co-operation and encouragement create workplace synergy. With this, team members are able to feel a greater sense of accomplishment, are collectively responsible for outcomes achieved, and individuals are incentivised to perform at a higher level.

    When team members are aware of their own responsibilities and roles, and know that the rest of the team is relying on their output, they will be driven to share the same vision, values, and goals. The result creates a workplace environment based on fellowship, trust, support, respect, and co-operation.

Leadership is a necessary element to promoting teamwork in an organisation. When leaders are great, there is a lot of positive teamwork and many benefits. However, when leaders are poor there can be negative consequences.

In business, leaders have the responsibility to do what they reasonably can to promote a good team environment. Practising team-oriented leadership strategies can do a lot to usher in a sense of teamwork among professional team members. It is up to the leaders to make sure teams are functioning to their highest capacity. Although it sounds like a large responsibility, the benefits of promoting teamwork are incredible.

PART THREE

Company growth and planning

CHAPTER TWENTY-TWO

Quantity or quality?

'Knowledge comes, but wisdom lingers. It may not be difficult to store up in the mind a vast quantity of facts within a comparatively short time, but the ability to form judgements requires the severe discipline of hard work and the tempering heat of experience and maturity'
– lawyer and US president Calvin Coolidge

While businesses tend to want as many clients as they can get, what good would getting the client be without the ability to retain them? If a business is busy taking on too many projects to produce quality products and services for their client, it's likely that they will lose them. On the other hand, if a business paces itself and spends quality time making new connections and building relationships, they are more likely to retain the relationships and be able to move forward with the next ones.

Even though large quantities can appear as an alluring and successful sign of business, it's easy to imagine how many clients of a quantity-focused company are not satisfied with its product or service and will not return to or stay with the company.

Taking the time to build rapport with clients will increase your company's substantial business, in turn building your company's brand and clients' trust. In a competitive business world, quality leads to quantity.

Michael Simmons' Forbes article "The most important decision you need to make when building a network", tackles, I feel, the questions we are all wondering when it comes to establishing relationships.

Initially, growth is both essential and inevitable. But at what point does expansion begin to hinder progress? Research by Harvard Kennedy School shows that after immense growth it is essential to re-evaluate your network. Once you have reached capacity, a large-scale network becomes inefficient, and difficult to maintain. In order to combat this, it is important to understand that as networks increase in size, quality becomes much more important than quantity.

Instead of forcing expansion, it becomes more beneficial to establish close, valuable relationships. At that point, you must decide which relationships are most important so that you are best able to foster and encourage their growth.

Focusing on quality should be foundational for any business and extend from the design of the website right through to the latest product that hits the shelves. The quality vs quantity debate can be relevant to every aspect of your business. Do you want to optimise your sales processes, marketing efforts, employee happiness and every other attribute of your business? Of course you do.

Here are five tips to increase business while maintaining quality relationships:

- Increase sales with higher quality leads

  The quality of your customer data affects every subsequent step in your buyer pipeline. It's about more than just accuracy. Low quality leads waste your team's time on research, data entry and chasing dead ends. High quality leads facilitate better reporting, automation and segmentation

- Ensure all products/services are flawless

  One quality product or service is often worth at least 100 mediocre alternatives. Have you ever noticed that luxury boutiques have many fewer shelves than the big-box stores? Not only do boutiques usually have higher quality, but they also have more loyal customers, higher sales points and are generally a much more reasonable venture for a start-up or the small business owner

- Don't take SEO shortcuts.

  If you know about search engine optimisation (SEO), you have probably heard about black hat tricks. These are illegal moves to falsely bolster the apparent popularity of a website, and they are almost always a short-term hack until search engine algorithms catch them and penalise them. A common trick is duplicate content and/or duplicate sites. You might suppose having multiple sites with the same content can boost your SEO rankings, but it can ultimately be your undoing. Focus on one very high quality site instead of several lower quality ones

- Nurture relationships with premium employees

  Both highly skilled employees and mediocre ones may leave your company, but the loss of top employees could hurt much more. You know who your most talented workers are, so do what it takes to keep them long term. Offer workplace programmes and benefits that show you respect their personal growth and long-term professional goals. This will help to ensure they don't move on before you expect

- Go with targeted marketing campaigns

  Be a sharpshooter with your marketing. It's more effective to take the time to research, pinpoint and create a marketing campaign for an appropriate demographic rather than pay for thousands of inserts in the biggest newspaper in town. It's the difference between hunting your prey in the wild and setting up for that perfect shot, or wildly shooting a machine gun into the woods.

Quantity versus quality applies to almost everything in your business. When you think of quantity versus quality what comes to mind for you?

When I think about quantity I think about things like McDonald's – fast food, cramped restaurant environments, inexpensive, fast paced, high volume.

When I think of quality I think about The Cinnamon Club – slow, nice high-quality environment, higher price point, more luxurious, more elegant. The reality of those differences is what makes one a quality experience versus a quantitative experience.

Quantity is really important – it may not be very exciting, but if you learn to get intimate with your numbers and you learn how to break them down, your quantitative numbers will show you a direct correlation to qualitative behaviour that can drive the quantitative results.

CHAPTER TWENTY-THREE

If you can tweet, you can become president

'Today's most respected and successful leaders are able to transform fear of the unknown into clear visions of whom to serve, core strengths to leverage and actions to take. They enable us to pierce the veil of complexity and identify the single best vantage point from which to examine our complex roles. Only then can we take clear, decisive action'
– First, Break All the Rules author
Marcus Buckingham

I was having a fascinating discussion with a CEO of a technology company around leadership, the weaknesses of being an ineffective social media presence and the CEO's communication to their stakeholders, when the president of the United States of America came to mind.

It's bizarre, really, but the fact is: Donald Trump is the first Twitter president of the United States of America.

In an interview with Tucker Carlson of Fox News recently, Trump put into words what many people have long been suspecting: that were it not for his mastery of hyperbole in 140 characters, he would not now be occupying the most powerful office on Earth.

"Let me tell you about Twitter," the president began, "I think that maybe I wouldn't be here if it wasn't for Twitter."

Combining his followers of his @realDonaldTrump and @Potus accounts on Twitter, Facebook and Instagram, Trump has the combined ability to publish directly to as many as 100million people.

All jokes aside, while the truth maybe the fact that Twitter, Facebook, Instagram and other platforms may attract his following of interested fans, the question you need to ask yourself is exactly what is his presidency costing the US, just as you could question a CEO of a FTSE 100 company that used social media to obtain his or her position in the same way?

My company is often being approached by executive boards of companies that are questioning their existing leadership decisions in people. It is clear that people love the title of CEO, but do not necessarily have the skills and ability to make the change necessary to drive the company to profitability and growth?

Let's take a look at some basic facts:

- We are in the worst economic circumstances we have faced in almost 100 years

- It is forecast to get worse before we hit bottom

- There are many organisations that have already executed large scale reductions in the workforce, and they will be followed by others

- Layoffs, reductions in force, or whatever you want to call them, cause anxiety, trauma and lost productivity.

Here are some of the facts about poor leadership costing a loss in productivity to American businesses that I found in an article published by Harvard Business Review.

According a workplace report by Gallup, 50 per cent of working professionals in US merely put their time in at the office; 20 per cent often represent their discontent via missing days on the job, driving customers away or influencing their co-workers in a negative way. Only the remaining 30 per cent are committed towards their work. What's the reason behind it?Poor leadership, Gallup says.

While doing research for their book *Leading People*, the authors Renee Rosen and Helen Gurley Brown found that the current state of poor leadership is costing American companies more than half of their human potential.

Loss of human resources does not only mean employees leaving an organisation. That's the ultimate loss, but a big loss is when the employees are not being used to their full potential. Poor resource management is one of the key telltales of weak leadership and can bring a company down. No matter how experienced and expert your resources are, if they are not utilised correctly, they will not going benefit the business. This will ultimately lead to loss of resources; or even the loss of the company.

Successful leadership is all about having the right people, with the right abilities, in the right place, at the right time.

According to the same report by Gallup, poor leadership alone costs American companies more than half a trillion dollars each year. According to the Cost of Poor Leadership Calculator created by DDI, a leading firm that conducts corporate research, one poor leader costs a company around $126,000 over just one year owing to loss of productivity, and employee turnover issues.

Corporations are victims of the great training robbery. American companies spend enormous amounts of money on employee training and education – $160billion in the US and close to $356billion globally – but they are not getting a good return on their investment. For the most part, the learning doesn't lead to better organisational performance, because people soon revert to their old ways of doing things.

Few companies truly understand how much poor leadership costs them. While CEOs and executives understand the importance of effective leadership, the drive to improve it often lacks urgency because it can be difficult to quantify the cost. After all, leadership is very broad, and covers a range of activities and behaviours.

Boards and CEOs can be fooled into thinking that their leadership performance is good enough. But is it really? Research by management training provider The Ken Blanchard Companies found that the average company operates today with a 5-10 per cent productivity 'drag' from less-than-ideal leadership practices. This means companies are forfeiting on average more than $1million a year in untapped potential.

Leadership solutions firm Zenger Folkman's research uncovered similar findings: that a poor leader loses a company $1million a year or causes it to only break even, while an excellent leader increases profits by 20-50 per cent. These variances may seem a little extreme, but they result in the same conclusion: that great leaders create more economic value compared to poor leaders who have a tendency to destroy it.

In another survey, The Conference Board CEO Challenge run by the think-tank The Conference Board, more than 1,000 respondents indicated that human capital is their top challenge, with customer relationships rising in importance in the past two years. Also, operational excellence and innovation remain vitally important for driving business growth and ensuring a sustainable future. These challenges (albeit varying in order) were the top challenges in all four regions included in the survey: the US, Latin America, Europe, and Asia.

When asked about the strategies they are adopting to address their human capital challenge, CEOs focused on leadership. Improving leadership development programmes, enhancing the effectiveness of senior management teams, improving the effectiveness of frontline supervisors and managers, and improving succession planning were four of the strategies in the top 10. CEOs know their organisations cannot retain highly engaged, high-performing employees without effective leaders who can manage, coach, develop, and inspire their multi-generational, globally dispersed, and tech-savvy teams.

CEOs also were asked to identify the leadership attributes and behaviours most critical to success as a leader.

The top five prominent in every region globally were:

- Retaining and developing talent

- Managing complexity

- Leading change

- Leading with integrity

- Having an entrepreneurial mind-set

So, how can leadership improve? First, leadership capability efforts are not always hardwired to business strategy. This will leads to initiatives that are disconnected and inconsistent across the organisation, diluting the overall focus on core leadership behaviours and cultural and business change. Without properly aligning current leadership capability against business goals, you miss the opportunity to identify key gaps, running the risk of focusing on the wrong things.

Second, focus is almost always on quality of content; how well we execute takes a back seat. This becomes even more difficult when you are trying to scale efforts across the enterprise or across different countries and cultures. According to the Corporate Leadership Council, one-third of a leadership programme's success is related to content and two-thirds are determined by the quality of the implementation.

Finally, despite the best of intentions, many efforts produce no lasting change in terms of behaviour and results. Don't be drawn in by the hype of five-minute videos and digitised options. This type of learning can be engaging, but, like a quick-fix diet, it doesn't work.

Failure to examine the big data and analytics to help understand (and react to) the gap between existing leadership practices and proven value to the business is a detriment to leadership development efforts. Too often we are still content with the smile sheets and anecdotal data. To be effective, we all need data-driven analyses to execute informeddecision-making processes and in real time.

My business partner in the US, Mark Herbert, and I created a checklist of priorities that should be considered when making change.

Mistakes often made include:

• Leadership development has long been viewed as a cost. It is an investment in your leaders and your business

• The programme is not adopted across the enterprise. If you do not predict and act on issues across geographies and cultures, there will be no consistency and implementation will not succeed

• Development is seen as an isolated training event or the 'initiative of the month'. That is ineffective if you're trying to achieve lasting behaviour and change. Reinforce learning and sustain the momentum by investing energy and resources to diagnose your leaders and guide them through a targeted journey of experiences.

CHAPTER TWENTY-FOUR

Is the world really out of control?

'It was the best of times, it was the worst of times, it was the age of wisdom, it was the age of foolishness, it was the epoch of belief, it was the epoch of incredulity, it was the season of light, it was the season of darkness, it was the spring of hope, it was the winter of despair, we had everything before us, we had nothing before us'
– author Charles Dickens (in *A Tale of Two Cities*)

After yet another shooting atrocity in America, the question, macabre but inevitable, arises again: "How do we respond to a world that seems out of control?"

According to The World Health Organisation, the world and its people are changing and losing knowledge. Females and males are losing their virginity as early as 10 years old. The crime rate is increasing daily. Every tenth of a second a crime takes place somewhere in this world. Children are disobeying their parents, teachers have no control over the behaviour of children, mental health is at an all-time high in every society in the world.

Entire countries are poor, and diseases eating away at their populations. Bad weather is increasing. Meteors hitting the Earth are increasing, hurricanes and tornadoes are more frequent, the summers are hotter than usual and the winters colder. Earthquakes are happening in places where there are not even fault lines. Wild fires across the globe are destroying many many acres of land.

The ozone hole is getting bigger, oil prices are rising and oil reserves are getting lower each day. The prices of goods and services are rising and the value of the world currency is lowering. Many new hurtful laws being created and more and more people are experiencing some type of illness.

Have these things been happening all throughout history and no one realised, or are things actually getting worse, making people pay attention?

The world can seem out of control. The sun rises whether you want it to or not, the toaster breaks, someone cuts you up on your way to work. But, actually, we've never had control. We have the illusion of control when things go the way we think they should. And when they don't, we say we have lost control, and we long for some sort of different state, where we imagine we'll have control again. But what we really want is peace. We think that by having control or becoming 'enlightened' (and no one knows what that means) we'll find peace.

All around us things are changing. People are talking about disruption: personal lives being disrupted, businesses being disrupted, society being disrupted. This disruption, this change, is coming from lots of directions: technology, things that are happening in the world, connected globalisation, urbanisation, changing and ageing demographics, refugee problems, politics, terrorism, the mobility of people, climate change.

Fear tends to dominate. Some people find themselves and their organisations feel frightened because they don't see opportunities, or they focus on the things that go wrong and are risky. How people react in uncertain moments is a good indicator of how they will react in the future.

Digital transformation is one of the largest changes of our time, translated into business model disruption, new services, cybercrime and new devices in an app- or bot-centric world. It also disrupts our ability to cultivate new multi-generational talent and respond to a rapidly changing marketplace. We create more data than people can consume. We used to talk about innovation trends as if they were in silos. Trends are still important, and have impact by themselves, but their combined impact is be much greater. We need to change how we think about business to remain successful and productive as individuals and as organisations.

We can see it happening all around us as accessible, affordable, adaptable technologies change the way we live and work, and become so fundamental to our lives that they shift our understanding of what it means to be human. The adoption of new technologies is accelerating, and technological breakthroughs are speeding up. It took radio 38 years to reach 50 million users, TV 13 years, the iPod four years, the internet three, Facebook one and Twitter just nine months.

While the digital economy holds great opportunity, it also brings new risks and challenges. So, what's at stake?

To understand the future, we need to look at the past. Half a century ago, the life expectancy of a firm in the Fortune 500 was around 75 years. Now it's less than 15 and declining. Of the Fortune 500 companies that existed in 1955, 88 per cent have disappeared since the year 2000. Only 60 remain. They went broke, they were taken over, they merged or they were split into pieces. In five to 10 years from now, a large portion of today's companies will probably have an offering that doesn't exist yet. Companies are going to change massively, and the rate of change is accelerating.

Maybe Charles Dickens had a point.

CHAPTER TWENTY-FIVE

Do we have international differences in corporate governance and conduct?

'Business continuity and planning is just as important for small companies as it is for large corporations. Plans need to be simple but effective, comprehensive but tailored to the needs of the organisation. Employers have a responsibility to their staff for their safety and security, and we all share the desire to ensure that any disaster or incident – whether natural or otherwise – has a minimal effect on the economic well-being of the country'

– UK home secretary David Blunkett

There has been much discussion of late on the values of corporate governance in companies, and, more importantly, the international differences in governance and agenda. As we both advise on company boards, I decided to speak to my business partner in the US, Mark Herbert, and create some joint thoughts on the matter.

Some of the questions we discussed were: How do you know a board is effective? Do you balance trust with challenging discourse? Is the CEO engaged enough with the board? How can the board challenge management with critical questions without engagement and collaboration? Do you engage in a continuous improvement process?

As you can imagine, our discussions were quite heated on leadership, and, at times, on the lack of engaged leadership in business today.

We looked at whether there is such a thing as a typical board of directors, since size and composition will vary according to a company's needs.

Board size can range from five to 18 members, although the average board size across Europe stands at about nine members. Regardless of size, there are certain practices that should be followed to achieve optimal results. Overall, it is important to establish the desired board profile for your company by identifying the types of directors needed in relation to your business goals and ambition.

The composition of boards continues to be a focus for investors, and companies areresponding by paying increased attention both to who sits on their boards and to enhancing their disclosure and engagement with investors. The data reported in the 2016 Spencer Stuart Board Index on Standard & Poor 500 boards highlights emerging practices, compiled from proxy disclosure and a related survey. Overall, the trends have stayed steady from last year but represent a meaningful departure from 10 years earlier.

Directors sit on an average of 2.1 boards, the index found. Nearly three-quarters (74 per cent) of boards have an over-boarding policy to limit the total number of boards on which directors may serve; 76 per cent set it at three or four boards. Only 43 per cent of CEOs serve on one or more outside boards, the same as the previous year, but more than a 10 per cent decrease from 10 years earlier.

Many companies regularly review the list of skills that are desirable on the board and match them with board members' profiles. Directors' 'softer' skills and personalities should not be forgotten as they are instrumental in establishing appropriate board dynamics. When deciding on the composition of your board of directors, you should keep in mind the balance between the number of executive directors (board members who are part of the company's executive team) and non-executive directors (board members who are not part of the company's executive team). You may also want to consider having independentnon-executive directors on the board.

According to Spencer Stuart, on average, 49 per cent of board seats in Europe are held by independent non-executive directors. Such directors can bring real value to a company by providing new business opportunities and independent, objective advice. They also can provide constructive criticism beyond that that comes from within the company. When thinking about your board's profile, you should keep in mind the practicalities related to the size of the board. In other words, consider that the effectiveness of a discussion is impaired when there are too many people around the table. Larger boards of directors are not always the best source of constructive challenge or fresh ideas.

Common convention suggests that a board size of between seven to 10 directors is optimal for most companies. Equally important is the issue of gender balance. This issue has received a lot of attention recently, since women tend to be under-represented on boards. In Europe, in particular, Spencer Stuart confirm this issue is pertinent, since only about 12 per cent of boards have a female board member.

While public attention mostly focuses on governance for larger and listed companies, many business leaders of smaller companies understand that the fundamental principles of corporate governance, such as transparency, responsibility, accountability and fairness, are beneficial to all companies, regardless of listing status or size.

Corporate governance is crucial for increasing an SME's ability to attract funding from both direct investment and credit institutions. Good governance is particularly important to shareholders of unlisted SMEs. In most cases, these shareholders are less protected by regulators, have limited ability to sell their shares, and are dependent on controlling shareholders. Accordingly, the higher risk implicit in owning a stake in an unlisted company increases the demand for a good governance framework.

Positive corporate governance changes have the impact of improving access to investment, allowing a company to access facilities of equity and debt. There has also been the additional impact of helping the company position itself for an eventual exit, trade sale or IPO, as the changes help send a signal to the market about the firm's emphasis on good governance.

Corporate management is the general process of making decisions within a company. Corporate governance is the set of rules and practices that ensure that a corporation is serving all of its stakeholders. According to the Center for International Private Enterprise, "Successful development efforts demand a holistic approach, in which various programmes and strategies are recognised for their important contributions to progress and prosperity. In this regard, linkages between corporate governance and development are crucial... Yet, corporate governance and development are strongly related. Just as good corporate governance contributes to the sustainable development prospects of countries, increased economic sustainability of nations and institutional reforms that come with it provide the necessary basis for improved governance in the public and private sector.

"Alternatively, corporate governance failures can undermine development efforts by misallocating much-needed capital and resources, and developmental fallbacks can reinforce weak governance in the private sector and undermine job and wealth creation."

Globalisation of finance and trade has supported the widespread adherence to common underlying corporate governance principles. They are not always country-specific, and have been applied in various and diverse emerging markets, adjusted for local regulations and business traditions.

Building a strong board of directors never seems to get easier. High-profile board failures, the boom in activist investing, and the disruptive forces of technology are only a few of the reasons effective board governance is becoming more important.

Start with oversight, a role of the board that, most directors would agree, is no longer its sole function. Directors are now required to engage more deeply on strategy, digital, M&A, risk, talent, IT, and even marketing. Factor in complexities relating to board composition, culture, and time spent – not to mention social, ethical, and environmental responsibilities – and the degree of difficulty in business is set to continue to rise.

Mark and I came up with a few points to help CEOs and board chairs, as well as executives and directors, build stronger boards. This synthesises multiple areas to make quick sense of complex issues in corporate governance, while focusing on the areas that are essential for building a better board and ultimately a better company:

- Corporate management development

    Corporate management has changed over time as managers have acquired better tools for understanding the problems they face. Most corporate managers are able to quantify many of the issues they consider, in order to make the correct decision. Managers factor in costs, benefits and the uncertainty of projects they are considering.

    A good corporate manager is someone who can perform sustainable functions within the company they work for, while either maximising revenue or minimising cost, depending on the department. Since the principles of corporate management are so broad, there are often specific disciplines for different parts of a company. The way a sales team is managed differs from the way the accounting department is managed

- History of corporate governance

    Corporate governance is a newer subject of study. In the past, many companies were run solely for the benefit of their managers or founders. A company might have outside shareholders, business partners and thousands of employees, but under older ideas of corporate governance, the company would pursue only the goals of its managers. Managers might choose to provide poor benefits for employees, knowing that these employees couldn't find better opportunities. Managers might also pay themselves excessive salaries without paying attention to community standards with respect to such practices

- Rise of corporate governance

    In recent years, many companies have become more conscious of the need for good corporate governance. As regulations have tightened, it has become more difficult for companies to exploit workers or harm the environment. In addition, changes in financial markets have made it harder for companies to harm their shareholders. A mismanaged company becomes vulnerable to being purchased by another firm, so managers tend to treat their shareholders better. An increased focus on sustainability as a business practice, not just an ethical position, has also affected corporate governance

- Measuring corporate management success

    Corporate management's success can generally be measured in terms of numbers. If the department in question is meant to create a profit (for example, if the entity being measured is a retail store or a factory), a quantity like profit margin or return on investment can demonstrate that it is achieving its goals. For departments that don't have such responsibility (like a shipping department, or an accounting group), many managers measure their results in terms of cost. If a department can accomplish the same functions and spend less money, then by this measure, it's a success

- Integrating corporate management and governance

  In recent years, many management thinkers have tried to synthesise corporate management and corporate governance into a single discipline. Since corporate governance is meant to equitably distribute the results of good corporate management, they fit together naturally; the best situation for a company to be in is for it to have good governance and good management. Combining these can take a variety of forms, from giving workers representation in company management to pursuing more efficient manufacturing processes in order to cut costs and help the environment. The most effective companies combine these practices in a mutually reinforcing way.

Mark and I discussed one more topic: trust. Trust is generally lacking when board members have begun to develop back channels direct to line managers within the company. This can occur because the CEO hasn't provided sufficient timely information, but it can also happen because board members are excessively political and are pursuing agendas they don't necessarily want the CEO to know about. If a board is healthy, the CEO provides enough information on time and trusts the board not to meddle in day-to-day operations. He or she also gives board members free access to people who can answer their questions, obviating the need for back channels.

Another common point of breakdown occurs when political factions develop on the board. Sometimes this happens because the CEO sees the board as an obstacle to be managed and encourages factions to develop, then plays them against one another. Pan Am founder Juan Trippe was famous for doing this. As early as 1939, the board forced him out of the CEO role, but he found ways to manipulate the senior managers at the company, and one group of board members he was returned to office. When he was fired again following huge cost overruns on the Boeing 747 that the company underwrote, he coerced the directors into naming a successor who was terminally ill.

According to Harvard University and its findings, most CEOs are not as manipulative as Trippe, and, in fact, they can be frustrated by the divisive, seemingly intractable cliques that often develop on boards. Failing to neutralise such factions can be fatal. Several members of Jim Robinson's American Express board were willing to provide the advice, support, and linkage he needed – but the board was also riddled with complex political agendas. Eventually the visionary CEO was pushed out during a business downturn by a former chairman who wanted to reclaim the throne and a former top executive of another company who many felt simply missed the limelight.

The CEO, the chairman, and other board members can take steps to create a climate of respect, trust, and candour. First and most important, CEOs can build trust by distributing reports on time and sharing difficult information openly. In addition, they can break down factions by splitting up political allies when assigning members to activities such as site visits, external meetings, and research projects.

It's also useful to poll individual board members occasionally. An anonymous survey can uncover whether factions are forming or if members are uncomfortable with an autocratic CEO or chairman. Other revelations may include board members' distrust of outside auditors, internal company reports, or management's competence. These polls can be administered by outside consultants, the lead director, or professional staff from the company.

CHAPTER TWENTY-SIX

Exactly what is the future in technology?

My vision for the future state of the digital economy – I see a movie. I see a story of everybody connected with very low latency, very high speed, ultra-dense connectivity available. Today you're at the start of something amazing… I see the freeing up, not just of productivity and money, but also positive energy which can bring a more equal world.
— chief executive officer – Vodafone,
Vittorio Colao

Technology forecasting is a completely unpredictable endeavour. No one wants to be a false prophet with a prediction so immediate that it can be easily proven incorrect, but long-term predictions can be even harder. Yet even though people know predictions can be a waste of time, they still want to know what's next. Wishy-washy tech timelines only makes prognostication more difficult, as entrepreneurs and researchers stumble around in the dense fog of developing prototypes, performing clinical trials, courting investors, and other time-consuming steps required for marketable innovation. It's easy to hit a wall at any point in the process, causing delays or even the termination of a project.

In the year 1820, a person could expect to live for fewer than than 35 years; 94 per cent of the global population lived in extreme poverty, and less than 20 per cent of the population was literate. Today, human life expectancy is more than 70 years, less than 10 per cent of the global population lives in extreme poverty, and more than 80 per cent of people are literate. These improvements are due mainly to advances in technology, beginning in the industrial age and continuing today in the information age.

One evening I brought together a group of distinguished individuals, including a global technologist friend of mine, for a 'great minds' dinner. This was the perfect opportunity to discuss what technology is working in the world, what is technology is emerging, what technology is not working, and, more importantly, what needs to change in order to accommodate all the prototypes of technology that seem to get stuck in the lab or on the shelf.

Thought leaders and so-called world futurists can dish out some exciting, and even downright scary, visions for the future of machines and science that will either enhance or replace activities and products that are near and dear to us.

Inventions like the VCR that were once high tech – and now aren't – proved challenging for some: the VCR became obsolete before many of us learned how to programme one. And who knew that working with atoms and molecules would become the future of technology? The futurists, of course.

Forecasting the future of technology is for dreamers who hope to innovate better tools – and for mainstream people who hope to benefit from the new and improved. Many inventions are born in the lab and never make it onto the consumer market, while others evolve beyond the pace of putting good regulations on their use.

There are many exciting new technologies that will continue to transform the world and improve human welfare.

The world around us is changing. In labs and living rooms around the world, people are creating new technologies and finding new applications for existing and emerging technologies. The products and services available to everyone thus expand exponentially every year. In the next five years, then, you can expect massive growth in what we can do.

Irrespective of the possible forecasting, I personally believe there are three imminent areas that will provide important developments in the next five years:

- Augmented reality will explode

  Technology mavens have talked for years about virtual reality and the applications available. Augmented reality is related, but allows us to lay the virtual world over the real world. Games like Pokemon Go provide examples of how this works; you use technology to 'see' virtual creatures and items in real spaces.

  Beyond fun and games, this technology provides a wealth of planning potential. You can drive your car, and arrows will appear on your road, guiding you. You can create visual representations of organising tasks, building endeavours, and almost anything else that you want to see before you start working. Manuals will virtually overlay real items to be joined together – everyone will actually be able to construct an Ikea bed! The technology is here; ways to use it are just beginning to emerge

- Mobile apps will decline

  At the same time, the ubiquitous world of mobile apps will begin to slip back. The ways in which we connect to the world often require us to work through a smartphone or tablet. The mobile app ties us to devices; you have no doubt seen rooms full of people who never make eye contact, only staring at small screens. The cost of developing sophisticated apps and the marketing efforts needed to place your app on the most expensive 'real estate' in the world does not always give a return on investment

- The Internet of Things will grow exponentially

  Availability and affordability of connected devices grow each year. We connect massive data networks to our homes, vehicles, and personal health monitors already. The ability to connect more devices, appliances and objects to these networks means companies will know more about those they serve than ever before. Almost any device with electronic components can be configured for the IoT, and in the next five years more will.

Berkeley and MIT researchers are pulling the present – sometimes step by step, sometimes by leaps and bounds – into the future.

The next few decades will feel this disruption, often in startling ways. Indeed, while the technical hurdles to advancing these technologies are fascinating, we see people writing about that the ethical and social dimensions of the changes they bring are the most interesting and troubling.

You can see how the allied sciences and complementary developments of these trends will reshape our world, our lives, and our work. Millions will find that the skills they bring to the table simply can't compete with smart automation. Legions of drivers, for instance, will soon find themselves unemployable.

And as AI continues to develop in tandem with robotics, the IoT, and big data, even the engineers and scientists who now design these systems will find themselves competing with their creations.

All of these developments will require you to examine closely not only what is possible, but also how privacy laws, intellectual property issues and the corporate ecosystems interact with those possibilities. Nevertheless, I am confident that within the lives of your grandchildren, so-called incurable illnesses will be beaten by bio, nano, and neurotech. And that 'ignorance' will become something children learn about rather than experience first-hand.

This technology is shaping things to come, and will define life for decades. Are you ready for the future? Ready to embrace the changes that are coming?

CHAPTER TWENTY-SEVEN

How to infuse boards with entrepreneurial spirit

*'A leader is one who knows the way, goes the way and
shows the way'*
– author and pastor John C Maxwell

During a 'meeting of minds' with a great friend, the subject of executive board management and entrepreneurial spirit came up, and we asked ourselves asking whether the mindset of boards can infuse entrepreneurial thinking objectively.

We all know that entrepreneurial spirit is a mindset first and then a behaviour. It is an attitude and approach to thinking that actively seeks change, rather than waiting to adapt to change. It is a mindset that embraces critical questioning, innovation, service and continuous improvement. It is about seeing the big picture and thinking like an owner; it is being agile, never resting on your laurels, shaking off the cloak of complacency, and seeking out new opportunities. It is about taking ownership and pride in your organisation.

Despite best intentions, too much success may ultimately lead to failure when employees in well-established companies focus on maintaining the status quo and following procedures instead of looking for new opportunities. Executives ultimately get a wake-up call when a svelte competitor swoops in and seizes market share by capitalising on an untapped opportunity.

Dr Glen Taylor, director of MBA programmes for global innovation at California State University, once said: "When things are going well, it's natural for companies to thrive on their own logic and nurture a culture that resists change, but if you don't consider new ideas and opportunities, eventually you'll hit a dead end."

Wherever you look in business, there's a new level of interest in entrepreneurship. As attention at corporations swings away from retrenchment and toward growth, more people are wondering why some companies and not just start-ups are able to stimulate creativity and initiative among their employees more effectively than others. Beyond helping to trigger the impulse, what do those organisations do to convert intriguing ideas into commercial ventures?

Most managers whose companies have found success in fostering entrepreneurial activity agree that no single practice enables them to identify and capture new opportunities. For example, many companies have found that pushing decision-making down into the organisation is only part of what's needed. Building a culture of entrepreneurship often requires pulling and nudging a variety of other levers as well.

Many large companies are seeking ways of reinventing or revitalising their entrepreneurial roots.

These companies often long for some of the spark, innovation, speed and risk-taking that they once had, but which have slowly eroded under the weight of size, bureaucracy, complex processes and hierarchy. Corporate entrepreneurship encompasses a set of activities, attitudes and actions that are believed to help large companies regain some of this lost magic. Although much has been written about corporate entrepreneurship over the last decade, very little is understood about its implementation within large company settings. First, the concept is little studied beyond the halls of academia, and there are very few guidelines regarding successful implementation.

The success of Amazon has forced Barnes and Noble to re-evaluate and change some key aspects of its business model. Homeruns.com has changed the way many people shop for groceries, and Autobytel has spurred GM and other car manufacturers to sell directly through their own websites, in direct competition with their own dealers.

What's going on? The little guys are taking advantage of the big guys, and the big guys have to fight back, fast. Entrepreneurship is quickly becoming the weapon of choice for many of these large companies. It is an attempt to steal and inculcate some of the thunder from these little entrepreneurial start-ups.

Corporate entrepreneurship can be a powerful solution to large company staleness, lack of innovation, stagnated top-line growth, and the inertia that often overtakes the large, mature companies of the world. Corporate entrepreneurship can also be hugely positive, a novel approach to new business development that often sits uncomfortably, sometimes impossibly, next to the planning, structure and careful organisation many large companies have often built so carefully over the years.

Big companies are turning towards corporate entrepreneurship because they are not getting the continual innovation, growth, and value creation that they once had. Unfortunately, many CEOs look around their own company, and see very few entrepreneurially-minded executives. Perhaps they never showed up to work because of their dislike of large company bureaucracy and politics. Or those who did show up were either pushed out or learned to stop pushing. We may all love entrepreneurs, but large companies have a way of eroding their entrepreneurial underpinnings. In large companies, most managers are rewarded for minimising risk, following the rules, and performing their functional roles to the best of their abilities. They look forward to a predictable rewards and, in many instances, a fairly predictable bonus.

Most big company executives would be hard pressed to call themselves value creators. They are quota and budget watchers. They are planners and organisers and more rule adherents than rule breakers. Big companies have slavishly gone after waste and redundancy with, sometimes, spectacular success. But these machinations rarely create long-term sustainable value for the shareholders. It helps the bottom line, but not necessarily the top line.

So how then can a corporate leader try to re-establish this start-up kind of mentality in his or her large company where the organisation's sheer size and bureaucracy have managed to kill this type of behaviour?

Corporate venturing involves starting a business within a business, usuallyemanating from a core competency or process. A bank, for example, which has a core competency in transaction processing, turns this into a separate business and offers transaction processing to other companies who need mass processing of information. In some organisations, functions like product development are tasked with new venture creation. Ventures usually involve the creation, nurturing, and development of a new business that comes from within the old business, but represents a new product or market opportunity.

Intrapreneuring, first espoused by Gifford Pinchot III in 1985, is an attempt to take the mindset and behaviours that external entrepreneurs have, and inculcate these characteristics into employees. Sometimes the company wants every employee to act like an entrepreneur, but a more typical approach involves the targeting of a subset of managers to act as corporate entrepreneurs. Companies usually want this cadre of corporate entrepreneurs to identify and develop spin-ups (innovations in current businesses that can lead to substantial growth opportunities) or to create an environment in which more innovation and entrepreneurial behaviour is evidenced.

Organisational transformation is another flavour of corporate entrepreneurship, especially if the transformation results in the development of new business opportunities. This type of entrepreneurship only fits the original Schumpeterian definition. Schumpeterian growth theory has operationalised Schumpeter's notion of creative destruction by developing models based on this concept. These models shed light on several aspects of the growth process that could not be properly addressed by alternative theories. In this survey, we focus on four important aspects, namely: (i) the role of competition and market structure; (ii) firm dynamics; (iii) the relationship between growth and development with the notion of appropriate growth institutions; and (iv) the emergence and impact of long-term technological waves. In each case, Schumpeterian growth theory delivers predictions that distinguish it from other growth models and which can be tested using micro data.

If the transformation involves innovation, a new arrangement or combination of resources, and results in the creation of sustainable economic value. Clearly, some transformations meet these requirements, while others do not. Transforming an organisation by de-layering, cost cutting, re-engineering, downsizing or using the latest technology does not guarantee that the organisation will recognise or capture new opportunities.

Industry rule-bending is another type of transformation, but focuses on changing the rules of competitive engagement. John M Stopford and Charles Baden-Fuller labelled this behaviour 'frame-breaking change'. Toyota, for example, changed the rules of the game in the automobile industry by producing low-cost automobiles of exceptionally high quality.

As a result, US and European auto manufacturers were forced by Toyota and other Japanese automakers to follow suit. Thus, Toyota not only transformed itself, but also helped to start a wholesale transformation of the industry.

Companies can take a number of different approaches to becoming more entrepreneurial. AVCO Financial Services, a large international finance company, was a very organised, detailed organisation controlled by many governmental requirements in the management of their business. These governmental requirements demanded great attention to detail, complex systems, and daily financial reporting mechanisms. Not the usual stuff of entrepreneurial, fast companies. AVCO did not try to change the whole culture, or create a mass of internal entrepreneurs, nor dabble too far into corporate venturing, but nonetheless it was still quite entrepreneurial in what it did. AVCO has operations all over the world, but mainly in the Americas, Europe, and in Asia. Much of its innovation and branch operations experiments were done in Australia. First, it reasoned that Australia was far enough away from corporate headquarters in California that the experiments could be undetected for months. And even if sanctioned, the experiments were being done in that odd country down under that seemed so remote to many at headquarters that it didn't make much of an image on the corporate radar screen.

If innovation is the ability to recognise opportunity, then the essence of being an entrepreneur is being able to mobilise talent and resources quickly to seize that opportunity and turn it into a business. Particularly for big companies, the challenge is to find ways to nourish the activities that give rise to innovation while at the same time cultivating the ability to move decisively once an opportunity presents itself.

Finally, despite all of the aforementioned, when corporate entrepreneuring works, it can work spectacularly. And, if the company is serious and supportive of internal entrepreneurs, corporate entrepreneurship can be a powerful tool for innovation, growth, and personal fulfilment if approached thoughtfully and with courage of conviction.

CHAPTER TWENTY-EIGHT

Not just data… meaningful data that enables decisions

> *'Hard numbers tell an important story; user stats and sales numbers will always be key metrics. But every day, your users are sharing a huge amount of qualitative data, too – and a lot of companies either don't know how or forget to act on it'*
>
> – entrepreneur and Flickr co-founder Stewart Butterfield

I have been discussing with the board of a company that I represent as a non-executive director the subject of meaningful data and the value of meaningful data – as opposed to data and information – in making informed decisions across the business.

Most organisations recognise that being a successful, data-driven company requiress killed developers and analysts. Fewer grasp how to use data to tell a meaningful story that resonates both intellectually and emotionally with an audience.

Joseph Rudyard Kipling was an English journalist, short-story writer, poet, and novelist who once wrote, "If history were taught in the form of stories, it would never be forgotten." The same applies to data. Companies must understand that data will be remembered only if presented in the right way. And often a slide, spreadsheet or graph is not the right way; a story is.

Boards of executives and managers are being bombarded with dashboards brimming with analytics. They struggle with data-driven decision-making because they do not know the story behind the data.

Sometimes the right data is big. Sometimes the right data is small. But for innovators the key is figuring out which critical pieces of data will drive the competitive position. It is those that you should seek out fervently. To drill down to the right data, I suggest asking the following three questions: What decisions drive waste in your business? Which decisions could you automate to reduce waste? What data would you need to do so?

Information systems might differ wildly in form and application, but essentially they serve a common purpose: to convert data into meaningful information, which in turn enables the organisation to build knowledge.

Data is unprocessed facts and figures without any added interpretation or analysis, for example, 'The price of crude oil is $50 per barrel'.

Information is data that has been interpreted so that it has meaning for the user, for example, 'The price of crude oil has risen from $30 to $50 per barrel' gives meaning to the data, and is information for someone who tracks oil prices.

Knowledge is a combination of information, experience and insight that may benefit an individual or organisation, for example, 'When crude oil prices go up by $10 per barrel, it's likely that petrol prices will rise by 2p per litre' is knowledge.

The boundaries between the three terms are not always clear. What is data to one person is information to someone else. To a commodities trader for example, slight changes in the sea of numbers on a computer screen convey messages that act as information that enables a trader to take action. To almost anyone else they would look like raw data. What matters are the concepts and your ability to use data to build meaningful information and knowledge.

The ability to gather meaningful data is as important as the insights the data can generate. Those insights, the end result of any data collection, is what people see and judge.

The hard truth here is that bad data leads to bad decisions. Therefore, it is important to take the time necessary to build a proper data collection process.

Data is meaningful if we have some way to act on it. Otherwise, we are mere spectators. This is one of the most problematic aspects of the current fetish of data visualisation, which appears to treat data as an unquestionable justification for itself, rather than as a proxy for things that we actually want to understand or probe.

If we are satisfied with mere data, datasets or data visualisations as the end goal – rather than all the contextual complexity behind who, why and how it was collected, and what was excluded from the presentation – then we are letting ourselves be content with just one dimension, not four.

Data doesn't need to be numeric, digital or electronic; it is anything that helps you to make an assessment, and in many senses if it is non-digital it can integrate a whole host of other phenomena, providing a much deeper, if more complex, proxy.

A wonderful example of this was an air quality experiment led by professor Barbara Maher of Lancaster University. In the test, four houses had 30 potted birch trees placed directly outside their doors; and four households, acting as control subjects, did not have any trees placed outside. Levels of particulate pollution were evaluated by collecting dust particles that settled on television screens, which had been wiped clean at the beginning of the experiment, and comparing the two sets of households to see which had amassed more particulate. The experiment showed – viscerally, visibly and physically – that planting trees reduced particulate. It didn't require a digital sensor to be placed on the mantelpiece of each house.

Here are ways you can make your data more meangingful:

- DIY data

    One of the best ways to make data more meaningful is to make it yourself. Measure something – your body, your home, your neighbourhood – and it helps you to not only understand something about it, but more importantly to figure out the questions you want to ask and the hypotheses you want to assess. Measuring something yourself (the way your body temperature fluctuates; the cycles of noise in your neighbourhood) means you can better decide why and what you might do to affect or act upon it

- Collective collecting

    When you join with others to measure something, you make meaning by having conversations about the data you are collecting. Sense-making in this situation becomes a collective activity – you don't even need to be using the same measuring equipment; you just need to be able to talk with each other about what you're doing. "I'm measuring air quality," you say. "Well, I'm recording atmospheric humidity levels," says your neighbour. Have a discussion and you'll start to build up an intuition of how they correlate, or even better, look at ways of affecting them together, ideally for the better

- User experience

   The most important aspect of making data more meaningful is to experience it in situ. Even if you were not part of the process of collecting a dataset, if you put yourself near where and when it was captured you are far more likely to be able to integrate all the unspoken, ambient, implicit, informal and unrecorded metadata that datasets and visualisations strip out with their numeric authority. To stand in a space, whether that's a neighbourhood or a city, and experience its windy mess while simultaneously being able to interrogate, prod and effect a dataset provides you with the kind of multivalence that is crucial when constructing any useful meaning. You are far more likely to be held accountable, and to hold others accountable, for making use of the data in any decision- making process.

Most captivating storytellers grasp the importance of understanding their audience. They might tell the same story to a child and adult, but the intonation and delivery will be different. In the same way, a data-based story should be adjusted based on the listener. For example, when speaking to an executive, statistics are likely key to the conversation, but a business intelligence manager would likely find methods and techniques just as important to the story.

   In a Harvard Business Review article titled "How to tell a story with data", Dell executive strategist Jim Stikeleather segments listeners into five audiences: novice, generalist, management, expert and executive.

   The novice is new to a subject but doesn't want oversimplification. The generalist is aware of a topic, but looks for an overview and the story's major themes. The management seeks in-depth, actionable understanding of a story's intricacies and interrelationships with access to detail. The expert wants more exploration and discovery and less storytelling. And the executive needs to know the significance and conclusions of weighted probabilities.

Discerning an audience's level of understanding and objectives will help the storyteller to create a narrative. But how should we tell the story? The answer to this question is crucial because it will define whether the story will be heard or not.

As humans, we are by nature social creatures, and we have evolved distinctively compared to other species as a function of our increasingly social world. Stories have the power to help us understand meaningful information and, as a consequence, can shape our values, determine our prejudices, and influence our dreams. Religious texts are the epitome of this; vertically through generations and horizontally among co-habitants, the most powerful stories written in such texts are still impacting the modern world to this day.

The psychology of stories, particularly in aid of memory, is a topic of extreme importance in our new age of information overload. By definition, facts simply present data whereas a story's narrative provides context, which augments our understanding and drives valuable insights.

Using stories to remember – known as the Story Method – is a simple technique used by memory champions. The method's effectiveness is rooted in the use of narratives ability to aid the memory process, via the emotional aspect of a story which can engage more parts of the brain, making the story, and its elements, easier to recall.

CHAPTER TWENTY-NINE

What can we all learn from the cyber threat landscape of 2020 and beyond?

> *'We face cyber threats from state-sponsored hackers, hackers for hire, global cyber syndicates, and terrorists. They seek our state secrets, our trade secrets, our technology, and our ideas – things of incredible value to all of us. They seek to strike our critical infrastructure and to harm our economy'*
>
> – FBI director James Comey

Every year, as a co-founder and member of the Neustar International Security Council, I attend the Neustar Cyber Summit. This year the summit was held at the OXO Tower in London, and there were some very interesting findings from the summit which I would like to share.

Rodney Joffe, chairman of the National Information Security Conference, started to discuss where the Internet of Things fits into the equation.

"The first thing to recognise is that the Internet of Things is a new phrase for something that's existed for years," he said. "The only difference is scale. Sometime in the late 1970s or early 1980s, some computer science students wired a Coca-Cola vending machine to the internet. The students wanted to solve the problem of walking down three flights of stairs to the lobby only to discover there weren't any cold Cokes in the machine. It was one of the first devices wired to the internet, and anyone could connect to it and askfor the status of the Cokes. So IoT isn't really new. It's probably best defined as all of the devices that can be connected to the internet that don't necessarily look like traditional computers. Items like smart power meters, smart light bulbs and modern home thermostats, all the way to critical medical appliances and devices, jet engines and power turbines.

"Because everyone is now focused on the IoT, we're trying to develop rules around how all people, places and things interconnect. But millions of devices and things that are out there already are not secure, so we have to find ways of securing them and making sure that everything that gets added in the future is secure. It's no big deal if the Coke machine is wrong, but what if a nuclear-generating turbine goes down or if all the air-conditioning systems in a city go on at the same time because the smart meters that control the smart homes were compromised?

"The other thing to recognise is that the industrial IoT is much larger than the consumer IoT. The breach of Target customer credit cards started when network credentials were stolen from an air-conditioning filtration vendor that had serviced various Target stores. Those credentials were used to hack into Target's system, then install malware on a large number of the chain's point-of-sale devices. The end result was brand damage for Target that has reverberations today.

"The facts are that, in 2016, we saw a number of huge attacks – many that exceeded 1Tbps. In 2017, by contrast, we saw fewer large distributed denial-of-service (DDoS) attacks, possibly because hackers were finding little advantage in taking a company completely offline. Another explanation is that hackers were simply enjoying the success of the previous year's myriad of extortion and ransomware-oriented attacks, as well as the many DDoS associated data breaches.

"So far in 2018, however, the big attacks are back with a vengeance. Earlier this year we saw the largest DDoS attack ever recorded – 1.35Tbps – using a new type of attack called Memcached, which will be discussed later. Then, a 1.7Tbps DDoS attack was recorded. Previous amplification attacks, such as DNSSEC, returned a multiplication factor of 217 times, but Memcached attacks returned amplification records exceeding 51,000 times! In fact, the potential return from Memcached attacks is so large that they do not require the use of botnets, making them a new and dangerous risk vector.

"We are hoping," Joffe continued, "that these attacks will go the way of the Simple Service Discovery Protocol (SSDP) amplification attacks, which used the protocol designed to advertise and find plug-and-play devices as a vector. SSDP amplification attacks are easily mitigated with a few simple steps, including blocking inbound UDP port 1900 on the firewall. There are similar steps that organisations can take to mitigate Memcached attacks, including not exposing servers and closing off ports, but until then, Neustar is prepared.

"As you think about how to deploy in advance of a new year of cyber threats, here are the trends and activities most likely to affect your organisation. In anticipating the major cyber security and privacy trends for the coming year, you can find plenty of clues in the events of the past 12 months. Among the now familiar forms of attack, cyber hacks of major corporate systems and websites continued in 2018 and will inevitably be part of the 2019 cyber security scene. Many well-known organisations around the world suffered significant breaches this year. The single largest potential data leak, affecting marketingand data aggregation firm Exactis, involved the exposure of a database that containednearly 340million personal information records.

Beyond all-too-common corporate attacks, 2018 saw accelerated threat activity across a diverse range of targets and victims. In the social networking realm, Facebook estimated that hackers stole user information from nearly 30million people. A growing assortment of nation-states used cyber probes and attacks to access everything from corporate secrets to sensitive government and infrastructure systems. At the personal level, a breach into Under Armour's MyFitnessPal health tracker accounts resulted in the theft of private data from an estimated 150million people."

So, what can we expect on the cyber security front in the coming year? Joffe put forward these trends and activities as being most likely to affect organisations, governments, and individuals in 2019 and beyond:

- Attackers will exploit artificial intelligence (AI) systems and use AI to aid assaults

   The long-awaited commercial promise of AI has begun to materialise in recent years, with AI-powered systems already in use in many areas of business operations. Even as these systems helpfully automate manual tasks and enhance decision making and other human activities, they also emerge as promising attack targets, as many AI systems are home to massive amounts of data.

In addition, researchers have grown increasingly concerned about the susceptibility of these systems to malicious input that can corrupt their logic and affect their operations. The fragility of some AI technologies will become a growing concern. In some ways, the emergence of critical AI systems as attack targets will start to mirror the sequence seen 20 years ago with the internet, which rapidly drew the attention of cyber criminals and hackers, especially following the explosion of internet-based eCommerce.

Attackers won't just target AI systems, they will enlist AI techniques themselves to supercharge their own criminal activities. Automated systems powered by AI could probe networks and systems searching for undiscovered vulnerabilities that could beexploited. AI could also be used to make phishing and other social engineering attack seven more sophisticated by creating extremely realistic video and audio or well-crafted emails designed to fool targeted individuals. AI could also be used to launch realistic disinformation campaigns. For example, imagine a fake AI-created, realistic video of a company CEO announcing a large financial loss, a major security breach, or other major news. Widespread release of such a fake video could have a significant impact on the company before the true facts are understood.

And just as we see attack toolkits available for sale online, making it relatively easy for attackers to generate new threats, we're certain to eventually see AI-powered attack tools that can give even petty criminals the ability to launch sophisticated targeted attacks. With such tools automating the creation of highly personalised attacks – attacks that have been labour-intensive and costly in the past–such AI-powered toolkits could make the marginal cost of crafting each additional targeted attack essentially be zero.

• Defenders will depend increasingly on AI to counter attacks and identify vulnerabilities

The AI security story also has a bright side. Threat identification systems already usemachine learning techniques to identify entirely new threats. And it isn't just attackers that can use AI systems to probe for open vulnerabilities; defenders can use AI to better harden their environments from attacks. For example, AI-powered systems could launch a series of simulated attacks on an enterprise network over time in the hope that an attack iteration will stumble across a vulnerability that can be closed before it is discovered by attackers.

Closer to home, AI and other technologies are also likely to start helping individuals better protect their own digital security and privacy. AI could be embedded into mobile phones to help warn users if certain actions are risky. For example, when you set up a new email account your phone might automatically warn you to set up two-factor authentication. Over time, such security-based AI could also help people better understand the tradeoffs involved when they give up personal information in exchange for the use of an application or other ancillary benefit

- Growing 5G deployment and adoption will begin to expand the attack surface area

  A number of 5G network infrastructure deployments kicked off this year, and 2019 is shaping up to be a year of accelerating 5G activity. While it will take time for 5G networks and 5G-capable phones and other devices to become broadly deployed, growth will occur rapidly. IDG, for example, called 2019 "a seminal year" on the 5G front, and predicts that the market for 5G and 5G-related network infrastructure will grow from approximately $528million in 2018 to $26billion in 2022, exhibiting a compound annual growth rate of 118 per cent.

  Although smart phones are the focus of much 5G interest, the number of 5G-capable phones is likely to be limited in the coming year. As a stepping stone to broad deployment of 5G cellular networks, some carriers are offering fixed 5G mobile hotspots and 5G-equipped routers for homes. Given the peak data rate of 5G networks is 10 Gbps, compared to 4G's 1 Gbps, the shift to 5G will catalyse new operational models, new architectures, and – consequently – new vulnerabilities.

  Over time, more 5G IoT devices will connect directly to the 5G network rather than via a wi-fi router. This trend will make those devices more vulnerable to direct attack. For home users, it will also make it more difficult to monitor all IoT devices since they bypass a central router. More broadly, the ability to back-up or transmit massive volumes of data easily to cloud-based storage will give attackers rich new targets to breach

- IoT-based events will move beyond massive DDoS assaults to new, more dangerous forms of attack

  In recent years, massive botnet-powered distributed denial of service (DDoS) attacks have exploited tens of thousands of infected IoT devices to send crippling volumes oftraffic to victims' websites. Such attacks haven't received much media attention of late, but they continue to occur and will remain threats in coming years. At the same time, we can expect to see poorly secured IoT devices targeted for other harmful purposes. Among the most troubling will be attacks against IoT devices that bridge the digital and physical worlds. Some of these IoT enabled objects are kinetic, such as cars and other vehicles, while others control critical systems. We expect to see growing numbers of attacks against IoT devices that control critical infrastructure such as power distribution and communications networks. And as home-based IoT devices become more ubiquitous, there will likely be future attempts to weaponise them – say, by one nation shutting down home thermostats in an enemy state during a harsh winter

- Attackers will increasingly capture data in transit

  We're likely to see attackers exploit home-based wi-fi routers and other poorlysecured consumer IoT devices in new ways. One exploit already occurring is marshalling IoT devices to launch massive cryptojacking efforts to mine cryptocurrencies.

  In 2020 and beyond, we can expect increasing attempts to gain access to home routers and other IoT hubs to capture some of the data passing through them. Malware inserted into such a router could, for example, steal banking credentials, capture credit card numbers, or display spoofed, malicious web pages to the user to compromise confidential information. Such sensitive data tends to be better secured when it is at rest today. For example, eCommerce merchants do not store credit card CVV numbers, making it more difficult for attackers to steal credit cards from eCommerce databases. Attackers will undoubtedly continue to evolve their techniques to steal consumer data when it is in transit.

On the enterprise side, there were numerous examples of data-in-transit compromises in 2018. The attack group Magecart stole credit card numbers and other sensitive consumer information on eCommerce sites by embedding malicious scripts either directly on targeted websites or by compromising third-party suppliers used by the site. Such "formjacking" attacks have recently impacted the websites of numerous global companies. In another attack targeting enterprise data in transit, the VPNFilter malware also infected a range of routers and network-attached storage devices, allowing it to steal credentials, alter network traffic, decrypt data, and serve a launch point for other malicious activities inside targeted organisations.

Joffe expects that attackers will continue to focus on network-based enterprise attacks in 2019, as they provide unique visibility into a victim's operations and infrastructure.

- Attacks that exploit the supply chain will grow in frequency and impact

An increasingly common target of attackers is the software supply chain, with attackers implanting malware into otherwise legitimate software packages at its usual distribution location. Such attacks could occur during production at the software vendor or at a third-party supplier. The typical attack scenario involves the attacker replacing a legitimate software update with a malicious version in order to distribute it quickly and surreptitiously to intended targets. Any user receiving the software update will automatically have their computer infected, giving the attacker a foothold in their environment.

These types of attacks are increasing in volume and sophistication, and we could see attempts to infect the hardware supply chain in the future. For example, an attacker could compromise or alter a chip or add source code to the firmware of the UEFI/BIOS before such components are shipped out to millions of computers. Such threats would be very difficult to remove, likely persisting even after an impacted computer is rebooted or the hard disk is reformatted.

The bottom line is that attackers will continue to search for new and more sophisticated opportunities to infiltrate the supply chain of organisations they are targeting

- Growing security and privacy concerns will drive increased legislative and regulatory activity

The European Union's mid-2018 implementation of the General Data Protection Regulation (GDPR) will likely prove to be just a precursor to various security and privacy initiatives in countries outside the European Union. Canada has already enforced GDPR-like legislation, and Brazil recently passed new privacy legislation similar to GDPR, due to come into force in 2020. Singapore and India are consulting to adopt breach notification regimes, while Australia has already adopted different notification timelines compared to GDPR. Multiple other countries across the globe have adequacy or are negotiating GDPR adequacy. In the US, soon after GDPR arrived, California passed a privacy law considered to be the toughest in the United States to date. We anticipate the full impact of GDPR to become more clear across the globe during the coming year.

At the US federal level, Congress is already wading deeper into security and privacy waters. Such legislation is likely to gain more traction and may materialise in the coming year. Inevitably, there will be a continued and increased focus on election system security as the US 2020 presidential campaign develops.

While we're almost certain to see upticks in legislative and regulatory actions to address security and privacy needs, there is a potential for some requirements to prove more counterproductive than helpful. For example, overly broad regulations might prohibit security companies from sharing even generic information in their efforts to identify and counter attacks. If poorly conceived, security and privacy regulations could create new vulnerabilities even as they close others.

In summary, the question, considered by Joffe, is not whether you will be attacked. It is when, by what, and how badly your company's reputation or finances will be damaged. And one thing is sure in the uncertain world of cybersecurity – the wrong time to consider defence is after the attack has occurred.

CHAPTER THIRTY

Disruptive change is inevitable – change is constant

'Market fundamentalists recognise that the role of the state in the economy is always disruptive, inefficient, and generally has negative connotations. This leads them to believe that the market mechanism can take care of all the problems'

– investor George Soros

Change is inevitable. More and more organisations today face a dynamic and changing environment. The oft-heard rallying cry in today's organisations is 'change or die'. Survival in today's global economy requires organisations to be flexible and adapt readily to the ever-changing marketplace. Change has become the norm. It is as necessary for organisations to pay as much attention to the psychological and social aspects of change as they do to the technological aspects.

We live in an era of risk and instability. Globalisation, new technologies and greater transparency have combined to up-end the business environment and give many CEOs a deep sense of unease. Just look at the numbers. Since 1980 the volatility of business operating margins, largely static since the 1950s, according to PwC has more than doubled, as has the size of the gap between winners (companies with high operating margins) and losers (those with low ones).

Change is the one true constant in business, especially when it comes to operating a business. Having defined processes in place to effectively manage change can help companies sustain success.

In today's business environment, knowing how to successfully navigate these changes and develop appropriate and effective processes to properly manage such change is a must. It's virtually impossible for organisations to make sound strategic decisions and completely accomplish objectives when deprived of strong change management strategies. This is especially true in the world of project, programme and portfolio management, where obstacles and ambiguity are inevitable at every juncture.

Companies all over the world find that they have to continually make changes to the way they work in order to stay ahead of the game, be profitable, and be relevant. Often, the changes are externally mandated, internally conceived (or both), but the reality is that companies do have to evolve, change, or die. The global landscape is changing: businesses are moving to take advantage of new markets; organisations are restructuring to operate better, given the current market dynamic; competition is causing companies to radically change the way they do business.

The old business is not coming back – this is not just a statistic, it is a fact.

Companies operate in an increasingly complex world. Business environments are more diverse, dynamic, and interconnected than ever – and far less predictable. A study by Innosight, "Corporate Longevity Forecast: Creative Destruction is Accelerating", which I read recently suggests that 75 per cent of the Standard &Poor 500 will turn over in the next 15 years.

Many businesses that have 'done things the same way for years' are affected by disruptive change: the economy changes, the competition changes, products change, technology changes, customers change, employees change, vendors change, buying methods change, delivery methods change.

Disruptive change is coming, and the only question is whether companies are going to cause it or fall victim to it. Disruption is not easy, to create or to confront it.

Businesses need to grow continuously in one way or another to achieve and maintain success. Growth comes by making positive changes that promote growth and by responding correctly to external changes.

Organisations throughout the world and across the global markets also recognise the need to embrace 'nimbleness' and 'agility' if they are to survive in the long run. The ever-changing landscape, globalisation and global dynamics make it inevitable that companies have to evolve fast, repeatedly, and in a continuously improving manner in order to comply with regulations, collaborate with customers, and stay ahead of competition.

While awareness of the challenges associated with change is prevalent, there is also compelling evidence of the long-term benefit of being great at driving organisational change. Therefore, it is expedient to look at some of the reasons why change is difficult, so that we can deliberately tackle the reasons for change complexity.

Sustaining success depends on an organisation's ability to adapt. Why can some companies take advantage of any change the market brings, while others struggle with market-necessitated modification? The reasons why will differ for each organisation, but the question is definitely worth asking, especially in light of the fact that the pace of change is accelerating at the fastest rate in recorded history. Most companies find it hard to transform themselves in difficult circumstances.

Leadership needs to have a mindset that although change-ability (agility, resilience) is essential for the survival and growth of many companies, there needs to be a concerted effort to build capacity to lead change effectively, and to purposefully build a change friendly culture in a systemic manner. This means that change leadership or sponsorship becomes a leadership competency that is recruited for and developed in leaders in the same way that it is done for other competencies such as decision-making.

Companies most likely to be successful in making change work to their advantage are the ones that no longer view change as a discrete event to be managed, but as a constant opportunity to evolve the business. Change readiness is the new change management: change readiness is the ability to continuously initiate and respond to change in ways that create advantage, minimise risk, and sustain performance.

Organisations, and the people within them, must constantly re-invent themselves to remain competitive. Sustaining success depends on an organisation's ability to adapt to a changing environment. Senior executives recognise that in order to compete optimally in the current and future landscapes, their companies will be expected to do more for less in a more dynamic landscape with issues of globalisation, new market opportunities, and new ways of doing business. There is a recognition that the changes are going to increase and the demands for business benefits realisation will also increase. It is now necessary that leaders increase their ability to successfully implement strategies by increasing their ability to manage change, and that they leverage this change management skill to make it a competitive advantage.

If you're struggling, or your market is down, change management is especially critical because growing companies are not afforded the time to weather the storm of down markets or decreased demand. Offensive change when the company is doing well is a whole lot easier to manage than defensive change.

I am not suggesting that you overhaul your business entirely change your mission, vision, and values or abandon your product strategy with every minor bump in the road. I am suggesting, however, that the best companies, the ones that experience exceptional long-term success, are able to quickly recognise the need to change and make the tweaks necessary to help their business continue its growth trajectory.

Here are three tips that can help the journey of change easier:

- Top-down support from the CEO level through to the senior executives below the CEO is what ultimately drives successful change. When the changes are major, you need to create a burning platform scenario that will encourage a sense of urgency

- Clear, consistent, and transparent communication by all executives is critical to explain why the change is necessary. Throughout the change process, it's important to regularly and clearly communicate the reasons for change and reinforce that message to your team so they understand why you're taking the hill in front of you

- Quickly identify the senior team members who don't buy in, and encourage and support them to leave the company if they refuse to embrace change. This means you may lose some very good people who helped you get to where you are, but those people won't be as valuable going forward if they aren't willing to help you get to where you need to be.

Business is a little like the growth rings on a tree. Every year, something changes – it could be your product, your top competitors, your customers' preferences, or any number of things. The best companies adapt to those changes, reinvent themselves when change requires it, and find a way to grow – in good times and bad.

Successful organisations foster a positive attitude toward change by anticipating it and purposefully planning for it. Change must be addressed in an intentional, goal-oriented manner. Change is something that people should do, not something that is done to them. People are more comfortable with change when they participate in planning for or implementing it because they gain some sense of control, which reduces their fears.

CHAPTER THIRTY-ONE

Will globalisation actually happen?

*'Globalisation means we have to re-examine some of
our ideas, and look at ideas from other countries, from
other cultures, and open ourselves to them. And that's not
comfortable for the average person'*

– composer and musician Herbie Hancock

The age of globalisation began on the day the Berlin Wall
came down. From that moment in 1989, the trends evident
in the late 1970s and throughout the 1980s accelerated: the free
movement of capital, people and goods; trickle-down economics;
a much diminished role for nation states; and a belief that market
forces, now unleashed, were unstoppable.

There has been pushback against globalisation over the years.
The violent protests seen in Seattle during the World Trade
Organisation meeting in December 1999 were the first sign that
not everyone saw the move towards untrammelled freedom in
a positive light. One conclusion from the 9/11 attacks on New
York and Washington in September 2001 was that it was not only
trade and financial markets that had gone global. The collapse
of the investment bank Lehmann Brothers seven years later

paid to the idea that the best thing governments could do when confronted with the power of global capital was to get out of the way and let the banks supervise themselves.

Now we have Britain's rejection of the EU. This was more than a protest against the career opportunities that never knock and the affordable homes that never get built. It was a protest against the economic model that has been in place for the past three decades.

Extraordinary times are leading to extraordinary challenges. Linda Yueh, fellow in Economics at Oxford University, addresses these geopolitical challenges and demographic changes and how it will affect global economics and the asset management industry: "Modern humans have created many thousands of distinct cultures. So what will it mean if globalisation turns us into one giant, homogenous world culture?

"The importance of the tribe in our evolutionary history has meant that natural selection has favoured in us a suite of psychological dispositions for making our cultures work and for defending them against competitors. These traits include co-operation, seeking affiliations, a predilection to co-ordinating our activities, and tendencies to trade and exchange goods and services. Thus, we have taken co-operation and sociality beyond the good relations among family members that dominate the rest of the animal kingdom, to making co-operation work among wider groups of people.

"And so, in a surprising turn, the very psychology that allows us to form and co-operate in small tribal groups makes it possible for us to form into the larger social groupings of the modern world. Thus, early in our history most of us lived in small bands of maybe 50 to 200 people. At some point tribes formed that were essentially coalitions or bands of bands. Collections of tribes later formed into chiefdoms in which for the first time in our history a single ruler emerged.

"But two factors looming on the horizon are likely to slow the rate at which cultural unification will happen. One is resources, the other is demography. Co-operation has worked throughout history because large collections of people have been able to use resources more effectively and provide greater prosperity and protection than smaller groups. But that could change as resources become scarce.

"This must be one of the most pressing social questions we can ask, because if people begin to think they have reached what we might call 'peak standard of living', then they will naturally become more self-interested as the returns from co-operation begin to leak away. After all, why co-operate when there are no spoils to divide?

"If we try to draw some conclusions from the 'why' we can see high levels of global employment and any form of prosperity will elude us and big reductions of poverty in the emerging world will not happen quickly enough."

Obviously, it is important to consider conclusions such as Yueh's on where people are located what individual views about the economies in which they live are: how they see the problem, how they see their future, and whether the ambitions of different countries' citizens can be advanced by stronger, more co-ordinated action around the world.

If you were to ask Americans what America has to do now to sort out its economy, some would say 'cut deficits'; many would say 'cut taxes'; but most would say 'cut the foreign imports that are stealing our jobs'.

If you were to ask Europeans what their answer is, they would probably say 'cut the debt'; and some might even complain about the very viability of the Euro and Brexit.

If you asked the Chinese what their solution was for their best future, they would probably answer that they are a developing country so other countries should stop threatening them with protectionism and complaining about their currency.

If you asked the developing world, they would call for an end to unfair trading practices that ruin their basic ability to export and say that aid is unfairly being cut or withheld.

If I asked the question a different way, asking the citizens 'What do you really want to achieve as a country? I am sure that the answer would be very different.

In America, people would say the main issue for them is jobs and rising livingstandards for the working middle class.

In the countries of the European Union, people would say that Europe needs to get its young people into work and cut its high levels of unemployment.

In China, people would say they want to see more personal prosperity, and that means cutting the numbers of poor people and giving the rising middle class the opportunity to buy homes and access opportunities.

In many developing countries, people would tell you the problem was poverty.

Yet in the absence of a bigger vision of what can be achieved, the politics of each country inevitably pulls towards the narrow tasks and not the broad objectives.

So how can this wider debate contribute to global growth and collaboration? Bradford DeLong once wrote: "History teaches us that when none of the three clear and present dangers that justify retrenchment and austerity – interest rate crowding-out, rising inflationary pressures on consumer prices, national overleverage via borrowing in foreign currencies – are present, you should not retrench".

Yet in the absence of seeing a different and global route to greater prosperity, each country is trying, post-crisis, to return to its old ways. However, the security people crave will come not from countries clinging to an old world, but from reinventing themselves for our new interdependent world: Asia reducing poverty and building its new middle class; America and Europe exporting high-value-added goods by building a more skilled middle class; all undertaking structural reforms but in a growing economy.

This is the answer to those who travel today not with optimism but in fear. But there is no old world to return to: it has gone. The transition between epochs is always the moment of maximum danger. It is also the moment of maximum opportunity.

Against this backdrop of the seemingly unstoppable and ever-accelerating cultural homogenisation around the world brought about by travel, the internet and social networking, although often decried, is probably a good thing even if it means the loss of cultural diversity: it increases our sense of togetherness via the sense of a shared culture. In fact, breaking down of cultural barriers – unfashionable as this can sound – is probably one of the few things that societies can do to increase harmony among ever more heterogeneous peoples.

So, to my mind, there is little doubt that the next century is going to be a time of great uncertainty and upheaval as resources, money and space become ever more scarce. It is going to be a bumpy road with many setbacks and conflicts. But if there was ever aspecies that could tackle these challenges it is our own.

It might be surprising, but our genes, in the form of our capacity for culture, have created in us a machine capable of greater co-operation, inventiveness and common good than any other on Earth.

And, of course it means you can always find a cappuccino just the way you like it no matter where you wake up.

CHAPTER THIRTY-TWO

The keys to fulfilment: determination and perseverance

A man can be as great as he wants to be. If you believe in yourself and have the courage, the determination, the dedication, the competitive drive and if you are willing to sacrifice the little things in life and pay the price for the things that are worthwhile, it can be done.

– American National Football League player, coach and executive Vince Lombardi

Determination and perseverance were a way of life for me growing up, as some of you may have read in my first book, *Freedom After the Sharks*. Each of us is, to some extent or other, a reflection of the experiences of our lives. However, whether and how we succeed is determined at least in part by how we cope with those experiences and what we learn from them.

Everyone has a story, despite difficulties in family life and professional setbacks. The journey to success is in the learning; we all possess the determination, drive and skills to create a successful and happy life – the bigger question is if we choose to use these skills.

Change has a funny habit of teaching you a lot about yourself; it goes to the core of your own weaknesses, strengths and eccentricities. Leadership forces you to stay true to yourself and recognise times when you are at your best and worst; the key is to stay focused and to make decisions that lead to continuous improvement. Even though this may be small, incremental change, it is positive, and you can build on even though you might feel like you're in quicksand.

Business has taught me much about life and learning and the importance of sharing knowledge and life stories with my employees and associates. My hopes, fears, beliefs, values and dreams were tested to the limit. I learned that only the difficult things in life truly bring satisfaction, and that achievement is proportional to the struggle needed to get there.

There is a great quote by the Chinese philosopher Lao Tzu: "A tree beyond your embrace grows from one tiny seed. A tower nine-storeys high begins with a lump of earth. A journey of thousand miles starts with a single step." Taking the first step is hard. It involves taking risks, learning new things and getting to know new people. Making sure the direction is right can also be trying. But when there is no step, your vision or dream will not come true. Once you have made up your mind, take the first step, however small it is.

Each of us thrives on being successful, and in doing so we often forget the difficulties lying in the path to success. We set targets and want to achieve them right away, but we are humans and may fall short on those goals. Failure at the start can lead to frustration, and shatters the self-confidence you had at the beginning. You might consider giving upon your dreams because you don't feel that you can ever succeed in life.

Most of us are ambitious. We have hopes and dreams. We have big goals and fantasies of success. These are not just big ideas and empty words. We work towards these dreams on a daily basis. We fight, we struggle, and we make progress day by day. It's not easy, but there's value in what we are trying to achieve.

The problem is, we tend to lose steam as time passes. We start to falter in our devotion to a project and we arrive at a crossroads, where we consider giving up. This happens for a few reasons.

Success, despite popular belief, is not a one-way path or a straight line. It is a muddled road with various ups and downs, and you should navigate it with particular care. You might fall or get lost on your way. However, if you keep going, you will eventually reach your destination.

Have you ever wondered how some prominent personalities achieved great heights of success? What did those individuals do that set them apart from the rest of us? How did they stay positive, when faced with failure?

Determination and perseverance can be summed up to mean you are committed to your goal. Additionally, these qualities enhances the goal's value for you and intensify your motivation level. They lead you to wonderful findings, and broaden your knowledge of yourself and your goals.

It is a well-established fact that success is not achieved overnight. There is no such thing as get-rich-fast success in the world. The road to success is a slow and quite precarious journey at times. It takes hard work and time to build up and you alone are responsible for your progress.

Determination and perseverance are the keys to a successful life. If you keep determined long enough, you will achieve your true potential. Just remember, you can do anything you set your mind to, but it takes action, determination, persistence, and the courage to face your fears.

There are no guarantees in life and certainly not in success. The number of factors at play when determining success cannot be controlled. Things like luck, timing and other people are often out of our hands – and that's okay. Success shouldn't be measured by the external value we gain from our endeavours, but instead on the internal benefit we receive from actually delivering on what we set out to do.

A quote from Theodore Roosevelt comes to mind when I think about the individuals who struggle for what they believe in: "It is not the critic who counts; not the man who points out how the strong man stumbles, or where the doer of deeds could have done them better. The credit belongs to the man who is actually in the arena, whose face is marred by dust and sweat and blood; who strives valiantly; who errs, who comes short again and again, because there is no effort without error and shortcoming; but who does actually strive to do the deeds; who knows great enthusiasms, the great devotions; who spends himself in a worthy cause; who at the best knows in the end the triumph of high achievement, and who at the worst, if he fails, at least fails while daring greatly, so that his place shall never be with those cold and timid souls who neither know victory nor defeat."

For any endeavour that you may start, always remember why you started, and use that to fuel your determination and perseverance to finish it. Whether it ends in victory or defeat, the simple act of trying, of not giving up, is what makes our work worthwhile. I had the fortune of learning more about myself by being put into adverse circumstances than I could ever have learned about myself from a psychometric test or a new Oxford business book; it was reserves of inner self and energy that made the journey possible.

The question is always: How much do you truly want your dream and do you have the courage to pursue it?

Epilogue

*'Our lives are measured in choices we have made along the
path we call living, each compass point, a possibility, each
step, an opportunity, seemingly random, each decision moves
us inexorably in a direction both unknown and yet somehow
familiar for upon reflection, the strength we find in choosing,
or the surrender of letting all unfold leads us to the place we
started from when we made that first choice to be here again'*

– music theorist Richard Cohn

To extrapolate how people in the near future will make the transition to a new life of human and machine, we first need to understand how scientists, executives and everyday people will be deploying and using technology in their world today. Research has shown that the real issue is not simply that humans will be replaced by machines; as humans we need to be better prepared to fill the every growing number of jobs, opportunities and have a clear understanding of a growth mindset.

For years, the dream of many researchers was to create an artificial intelligence that could rival that of people. However, we are seeing that artificial intelligence is instead becoming a tool to extend our own human capabilities. As the fourth industrial revolution steams into the workplace, executives and people will need to assess various implications: How will job requirements need to evolve? How will and job displacements be balanced with broader workforce considerations? What new investments in talent are needed to retain industry expertise, and which employees many need to be counselled and retrained?

There are also government regulations, ethical design standards, such as those proposed by the IEEE, and prevailing public sentiment to consider. Companies will have a plethora of new laws and regional policies to take into account, such as General Data Protection Regulation (GDPR) and the Privacy and Electronic Communications Regulations (PECR), which will not just affect Europe; this will become a global issue as artificial intelligence becomes increasingly capable of deriving unprecedented types of insights beyond basic demographics.

The world will not be able to live with artificial intelligence alone. Research today has proved that companies that use artificial intelligence to augment their human talent while reimagining their business processes achieve step gains in performance, propelling themselves to the forefront of their industries.

I do not doubt that we are at a cusp of a new era of business and life transformation, the age of artificial intelligence, and our actions today have great bearing on how the future unfolds.

Which brings me to the heart of innovation creativity. Creativity has been described by many as a myth. As humans we all have creativity; the question is whether we choose to use creativity to drive outcomes in business or our personal lives for growth. Creativity at its core is about believing in your ability to create change in the world around you. It is the conviction that you can achieve what you set out to do. I have always believed this self-assurance, this belief in your creative capacity, lies at the heart of innovation.

After years of working with humans and technology, in my experience everybody has a creative gene; you can get individuals to stick to a methodology that will lead amazing outcome. Creative energy is one of the most precious resources. It can find innovative solutions to some of the most intractable problems.

People who use their creativity have a greater impact on the world around them, whether that means becoming engaged with their child's school, turning a storage room into a vibrant innovation space or office, or harnessing social media to recruit more bone marrow donors – it's all creativity.

As legendary psychologist and Stanford professor Albert Bandura has shown, our belief systems affect our actions, goals, and perception. Individuals who come to believe they can effect change are more likely to accomplish what they set out to do.

Creativity is a way of seeing that potential and your place in the world more clearly, unclouded by anxiety and doubt.

So, what drives creativity? History has proven that some of the most passionate, successful people are those who have sacrificed many of their needs to push toward one all-encompassing goal.

We all have different advantages, some based on good fortune and some based on choices we have previously made. We can only ever start from where we are. If we have the strength to play our hands, instead of questioning why we don't hold different cards, then we can decide at any time to work toward doing what we love.

The important thing is to remember that so much is still possible. We all deserve to enjoy the way we spend our days. If we're willing to dream, work hard, learn, and navigate uncertainty, we all have the potential to do it I was sharing coffee with one of my great author friends recently, discussing one of my books, *Meaningful Conversations*, and we talked about how to write life's tapestry if the heart is blocked.

The feeling I am describing is when you sit down to write and instead of feeling an energetic creative flow, you are paralysed, staring at your computer screen and seething at the injustice of your lack of creative life. Many people describe this as writer's block.

Studies have found writer's block to be a simpler problem: an inability to allow the creative process to flow because of unhappiness. This happened to me when I wrote *Freedom After the Sharks*. But there are different kinds of unhappiness, and it is the writer's job to be honest about which kind they're suffering from. In some respects, this can be a very important part of a writer revealing the truth about his or her unhappiness. The truth is always revealed in writing, as in photography, as author Robert Louis Stevenson wrote: "I doubt if these islanders are acquainted with any other mode of representation but photography; so that the picture of an event (on the old melodrama principle that 'the camera cannot lie', would appear strong proof of its occurrence."

Woody Allen makes fun of writer's block. He wrote a play called Writer's Block, and he wrote, directed, and starred in a film called Deconstructing Harry, in which the protagonist, Harry Block, tells his therapist. "For the first time in my life I experience writer's block... Now this, to me, is unheard of... I start these short stories and I can't finish them... I can't get into my novel at all... because I took an advance."

Writer's block immediately disqualifies Harry Block from being Woody Allen because Woody Allen is one of the most productive film makers of his and possibly any generation. Between 1965 and 2014, he was credited in more than 66 films as a director, writer or actor, and more often than not as all three. To take his writing alone, Allen has written 49 full-length theatrical films, eight stage plays, two television films and two short films in less than 66 years – a rate of a script a year.

I have studied Woody Allen, and when you look at his miraculous life you can ascertain that time was of the most importance to his every moment. This quote really says everything about his passion for writing: "I never like to let any time go unused. When I walk somewhere in the morning, I still plan what I'm going to think about, which problem I'm going to tackle. I may say, 'This morning I'm going to think of titles'. When I get in the shower in the morning, I try to use that time. So much of my time is spent thinking because that's the only way to attack these writing problems."

Allen had many philosophies that I admire, but I feel the one that resonates with me the most is intrinsic motivation: 'Self-motivation is the only motivation.' In life there are natural forces that we cannot guide or control, but I have learned as a writer that the power to create always comes from within. I often say, here in *Purposeful Discussions* and elsewhere, "Never, never give up on your dreams", "The truth always comes down to how much you really want to achieve your dream", and "Do you like the idea, or are your driven to achieve your idea?"

One of my mentors many years ago would say to me stop procrastinating and just do what needs to be achieved; I have never forgotten those words.

Writing is subjective, cach and every one of us has a distinctive view and preference when it comes to genre. As an author you will never please everyone, but with passion you can create your best.

Part of writer's block comes from fear of the unknown and worry about what others will think. Woody Allen spoke of why indifference is so important – something that we all can relate to in business today – when he said: "Longevity is an achievement, yes, but the achievement that I'm going for is to try to make great films. That has eluded me over the decades."

I believe every single person has passion for something. Passion, if directed in the right way, can create amazing things. But beware – passion focused in the opposite direction can destroy. So many of us, for reasons only we can answer, do not implement, execute or action our true and passion. Unfulfilled passion creates a cavity between our present and our true potential. You have all heard of the saying 'If only…' or 'It might have been different if…' Unfulfilled passion creates negative and malicious intent, which takes us away from our ultimate desires and purpose in life.

Author Steve Brunkhorst once said: "As we weave the tapestries of our lives, we gradually begin to see our designs from a wider angle of years. We may or may not be pleased with what we see. Yet, no design – not in the living world – is carved in stone. We have the gift of free will to change our designs as we wish. We are each a thread in the tapestry of our human family. Our outcome is woven of endless possibilities, because we can choose from a universe of endless possibilities. Every person can make a difference. Each thread is a possibility, chosen by the design of divine imagination. Our lifetime designs arise from our divine gifts, unique talents, desires, thoughts, choices, and actions. At times, old choices – old threads – wear out. We see the

past while we live in the present, and we can replace the old…
with new ideas, new choices, and new actions. We can view the
future through today's eyes, and time blends all experiences,
dark and light, into an awareness of authentic joy. May you live
joyfully and abundantly today and throughout every season of
life!"

Some final points on love and passion:

* Do what you love and the money will follow

  If there's one thing that holds us back from pursuing
  our passions, it's fear of notbeing able to take care of
  ourselves. It's what keeps us in unfulfilling jobs: the
  guaranteed salary.

  But this ignores the fact that succeeding in anything
  requires a great deal of work and uncertainty. Risk is
  always part of the equation. For everyone who has
  made a good living doing something they enjoy, there
  are countless other equally talented people who were
  not able to do it. This does not mean we should not
  pursue our passions; it just means we're more apt to feel
  satisfied doing it if we define success in terms beyond
  financial gain. That might mean we need to live on less.
  It might mean we need to balance our passion with
  other work.

  Do what you love and enjoyment will follow. Do
  what you love and you will feel more fulfilled. Do what
  you love and the money will seem less relevant. These
  things I have found are true

- Leap and the net will appear Fear can hold you back from making the leap, especially when you have no idea where you'll land or how. A lot of us get caught in the planning stage because we want to know with absolute certainty we won't make a mistake we'll one day regret. So we wait, we gather information, we imagine all possible outcomes and plan to avoid negative ones, and generally anchor ourselves with good intentions that, sometimes, never lead to action.

  We need to have faith that we won't fall flat on our faces. But the reality is that we sometimes we will. What's important to realise is that we are strong enough to get back up if this happens, and we can do it knowing that every fall is valuable. Every time a net does not appear, we learn a little more about how to weave one for ourselves. We also learn to be comfortable in the drop, which, if we're honest, is where we always live. Life is uncertain, whether we take large risks or not.

  It's not just the leaps that dictate our success; it's our capacity for soaring through the unknown, and our willingness to learn from the landing

- Do what you love, and you'll never work a day in your life

  With any job or business, you often need to do things you would not choose to do.

  But that's not the only reason doing what you love can feel like work. There's also the inevitability that most tasks feel different when they become things we need to do in order to earn. When the monetary compensation increases, suddenly the money becomes the motivation, and, as a result, it feels less enjoyable.

I suspect this comes down to freedom: we tend to best enjoy the things we feel we're doing entirely by choice. Since work, in any form, requires commitment that supersedes our moment-to-moment whims, we need to know when going in that even the most enjoyable paths will have their ups and downs.

I do hope my book has provided you with a better lens to understand the opportunities and challenges ahead, that you feel better able to chart your course for change and fulfilment of your dreams, desires and aspirations.

Society cannot flourish without some sense of shared purpose and belief system – and, most importantly, love. I am a firm believer in the power of curiosity and choice as the engine of fulfilment, but precisely how you arrive at your true calling is an intricate and highly individual dance of discovery. Still, there are certain factors and certain choices on your journey of life that make it easier and more worthwhile. Everyone has a story, despite difficulties in family life and professional setbacks. The journey of life is in the learnings, we all possess the determination, passion, drive, creativity and skills to create a foundation and happy life – the bigger question is if we choose to use these skills for the greater good.

ABOUT GEOFF HUDSON-SEARLE

Geoff is a serial business advisor, C-suite executive, and non-executive director to growth-phase tech companies, with more than 28 years of experience in the business and management arena. He lectures regularly and is a member and fellow of the Institute of Directors and an Associate of the Chartered Institute of Management. He holds a master's degree in business administration.

Rated by Agilience as a Top 250 Harvard Business School authority covering strategic management and management consulting, Geoff has worked on strategic growth, strategy, operations, finance, international development, growth and scale-up advisory programmes for the British Government, Citibank, Kaspersky, BT, Barclays, and various SMEs, among others.

Geoff is the author of five books, including the bestselling *Meaningful Conversations*. He lectures at business forums, conferences and universities, and his thoughts on leadership and authorisms have featured in the TEDx and RT Europe's business documentary.

QUOTES OF PRAISE FOR
PURPOSEFUL DISCUSSIONS

"One of the greatest challenges leaders face is being wholly 'on purpose' when they communicate, particularly toward the advancement of their personal and organizational vision. In Purposeful Discussions, Geoff Hudson-Searle's insights and advice serve as a beacon for executives seeking to achieve their goals expeditiously while being personally fulfilled along their journey."

Lisa Petrilli

Executive leader, strategic marketing and head of Medline patient experience & innovation institute

Medline Industries Inc

'Another great book by Geoff. His insights into the modern world of communication and developing strategy at the highest levels are both revealing and poignant for the turbulent times we live in. An essential book for both those in business and those travelling through the journey of life'

Neil Alphonso, Entrepreneur and Business leader

In his latest book, Purposeful Discussions, author Geoff Hudson Searle continues to reinforce the importance and critical role that face to face conversation plays in achieving organizational goals. His latest entry describes both the criticality of purposeful discussion and how those key conversations are distinguished from what passes for communication in this age of technology and immediate gratification.

Trust remains the foundation of high functioning relationship and can only be achieved by meaningful dialogue between the parties.....

Mark F. Herbert, Executive Director of New Paradigms LLC

Without a doubt in today's world communication has become key as the personalisation wave encompasses us. Geoff's book highlights the ever-increasing importance of framing those conversations correctly in business and in our social circles. Emphasising the importance of messaging, context and timing. A book worth of the read for all business people irrespective of how experienced you are.

Neil Currie, International Executive Director

"A refreshing insight into the real challenges that decision makers face in an increasingly dynamic and demanding business environment. Geoff has taken an honest look into how technology and human interaction co-operate and how this union can effect positive outcomes for us. A must read for anyone with an entrepreneurial mindset."

Michael Sharp DipPFS, ACII, Principal of Sharp Wealth Management, Associate Partner Practice of ST. JAMES'S PLACE WEALTH MANAGEMENT PLC

Purposeful communications and discussions have to be learnt as they are element skills of professionals. Geoff's book is an amazing, tool for us all to develop these skills. Don't stop learning keep earning!

Susanna Toth, CEO, H-Net Translation Agency, Associate Partner of Trade Bridge Group

There are very few people that truly understand how to have a meaningful and productive conversation and I can say the Geoff is one of those individuals. Active listening and the ability to communicate effectively is key to success. I look forward to reading the new book.

Scott Siegel, North America Delivery Leader – Insights and Data, Hitachi Vantara

For exclusive discounts on Matador titles,
sign up to our occasional newsletter at
troubador.co.uk/bookshop